P9-DJV-784

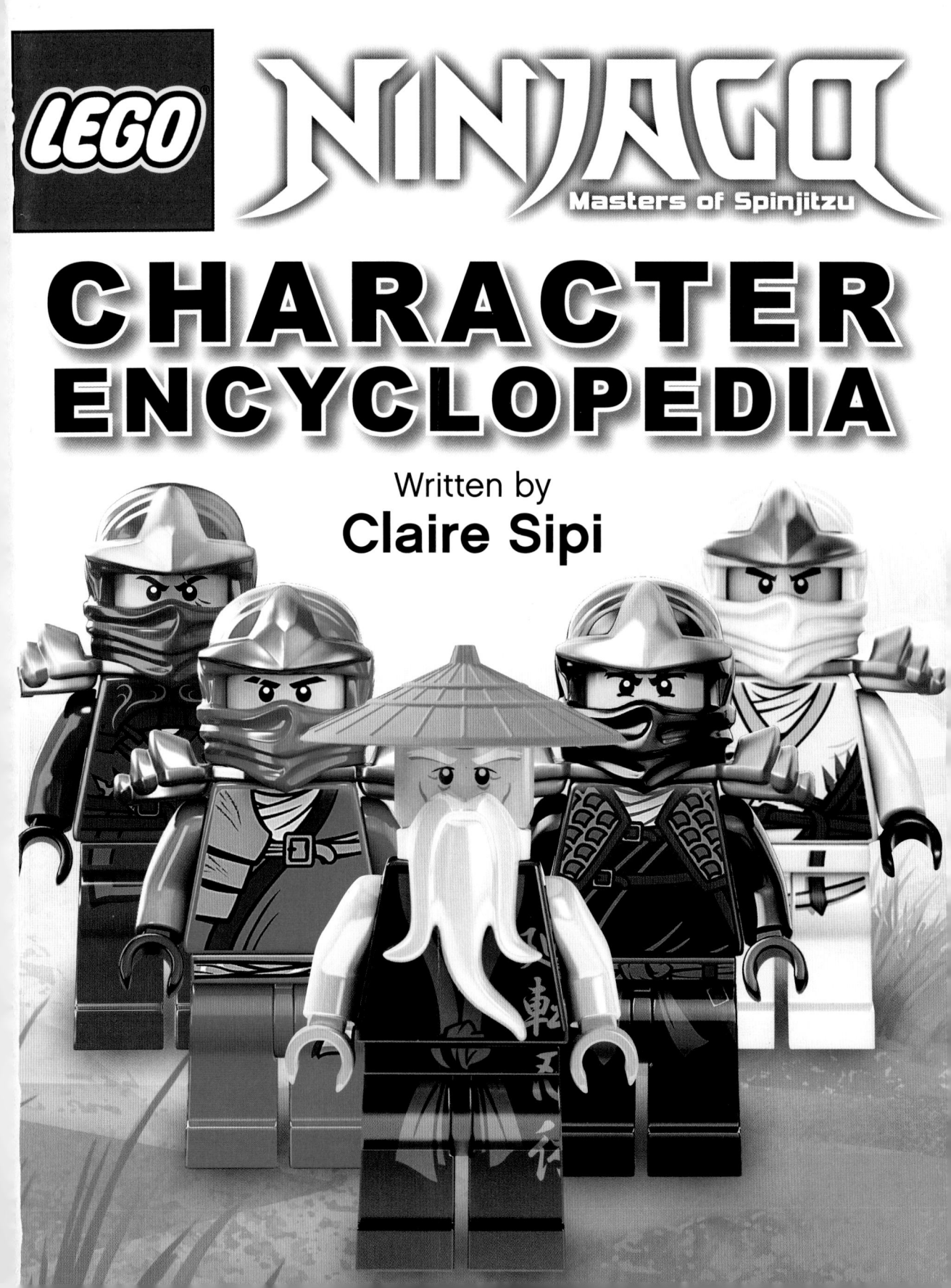
LEGO
NINJAGO
Masters of Spinjitzu
CHARACTER
ENCYCLOPEDIA
Written by
Claire Sipi

CONTENTS

4 Welcome Brave Ninja
6 History of Ninjago

NINJA VS. SKELETON

10 Lord Garmadon Returns
12 Meet The Ninja
14 Ninja Wisdom
16 Kai
18 Nya
20 Blacksmith Shop
22 Sensei Wu
24 Spinjitzu Dojo
26 Jay
28 Cole
30 Zane
32 Mountain Shrine
34 Training Outpost
35 Ambush Shrine
36 Fire Temple
38 Kai DX
39 Fire Dragon
40 Jay DX
41 Lightning Dragon
42 Cole DX
43 Earth Dragon
44 Zane DX
45 Ice Dragon
46 Meet The Skeleton Army
48 Skeleton Wisdom
50 Lord Garmadon
51 Samukai
52 Frakjaw
54 Turbo Shredder
56 Krazi
58 Chopov
60 Skull Motorbike
62 Bonezai
64 Ninja Battle Arena
66 Skeleton Bowling
68 Kruncha
70 Skullcopter
72 Wyplash
74 Skull Truck
76 Nuckal
78 Nuckal's ATV
80 Dark Fortress
82 Weapons
86 Final Battle At The Dark Fortress

NINJA VS. SERPENTINE

90 A New Adventure
92 Sensei Wu
94 Destiny's Bounty
96 Kai ZX
98 Blade Cycle
100 Jay ZX
102 Storm Fighter

104 Samurai X
106 Samurai Mech
108 Cole ZX
110 Tread Assault
112 Zane ZX
114 Ultra Sonic Raider
116 Kendo Ninja
117 NRG Ninja
118 The Green Ninja
120 Meet The Serpentine
124 Serpentine Wisdom
126 Lord Garmadon
127 Lloyd Garmadon
128 Venomari Shrine
130 Acidicus
131 Spitta
132 Lasha
134 Lasha's Bite Cycle
136 Lizaru
137 Fangtom
138 Fangdam
140 Fangpyre Truck
142 Fangpyre Wrecking Ball
144 Fang-Suei
146 Rattlecopter
148 Fangpyre Mech
150 Snappa
151 Skales
152 Slithraa
153 Rattla
154 Mezmo
155 Skalidor
156 Bytar
157 Chokun
158 Snike
159 Pythor
160 Snake Arena
162 Epic Dragon Battle
164 Weapons
168 Ultra Dragon VS. The Great Devourer

AND BEYOND...

172 Minifigure Gallery
174 Set Gallery
176 Acknowledgments

WELCOME
BRAVE NINJA

The world of LEGO® Ninjago is full of adventure, danger, and epic battles! Meet the four Ninja, Kai, Cole, Jay, and Zane, and learn about their various minifigures, weapons, and vehicles. Meet their first enemies, the terrifying Skeleton Army, and find out everything you ever wanted to know about these bony villains and their vehicles. If you dare, read all about the Ninja's second deadly foe, the Serpentine. Discover the secrets of this sinister snake army and meet all the evil Serpentine minifigures, from the smallest to the tallest.

To find out more about this minifigure see p.38

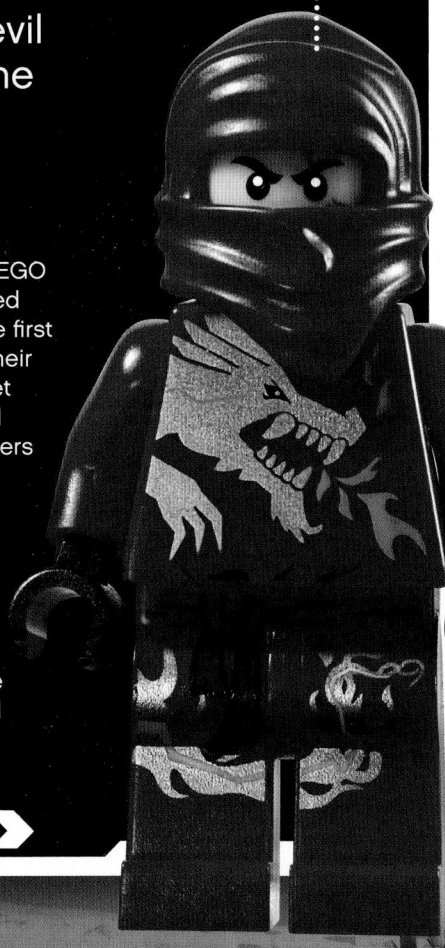

HOW TO USE THIS BOOK

This book is a comprehensive guide to every LEGO Ninjago minifigure, vehicle, and location released so far. Divided into chapters for each series, the first part of the book examines the 2011 Ninja and their locations, weapons, and dragons. Then we meet the Ninja's enemies, the evil Skeleton Army, and their vehicles. The second part of the book covers the 2012 sets, introducing the newest Ninja minifigures and locations, and their Serpentine enemies. Ninja Files in this section relate to the most recent set that the minifigure has appeared in, although he or she may have featured in more than one set.

The final part of the book has a comprehensive list of all the Ninjago minifigures and sets for all the fact-loving LEGO fans!

HISTORY OF NINJAGO

A very long time ago, the land of Ninjago was created by the first Master of Spinjitzu, using the four Golden Weapons. Stories tell of the mysterious energy of these Elemental Weapons whose combined power was so great that no single person could handle them all at one time.

The Spinjitzu Master told his two sons—Sensei Wu and Lord Garmadon—about the power of these legendary Weapons. He revealed that if the Weapons ever fell into evil hands, it would lead to chaos and the destruction of Ninjago. The Master said they must be protected at all costs, so when he died his sons swore to keep the Weapons safe.

While Sensei Wu was a good and wise person, his brother Lord Garmadon was evil and wicked. He wanted to possess the Weapons for his own terrifying purposes. The two brothers fought a terrible battle but Sensei Wu emerged victorious. Lord Garmadon was defeated and banished to the Underworld. Sensei Wu then hid the Weapons in the far corners of Ninjago, and peace returned. Until now...

DID YOU KNOW?

There are four Elements of Ninjago—Fire, Ice, Earth, and Lightning. Each Element is linked to a Golden Weapon: the Dragon Sword of Fire (Fire), the Shurikens of Ice (Ice), the Scythe of Quakes (Earth), and the Nunchucks of Lightning (Lightning).

SENSEI WU

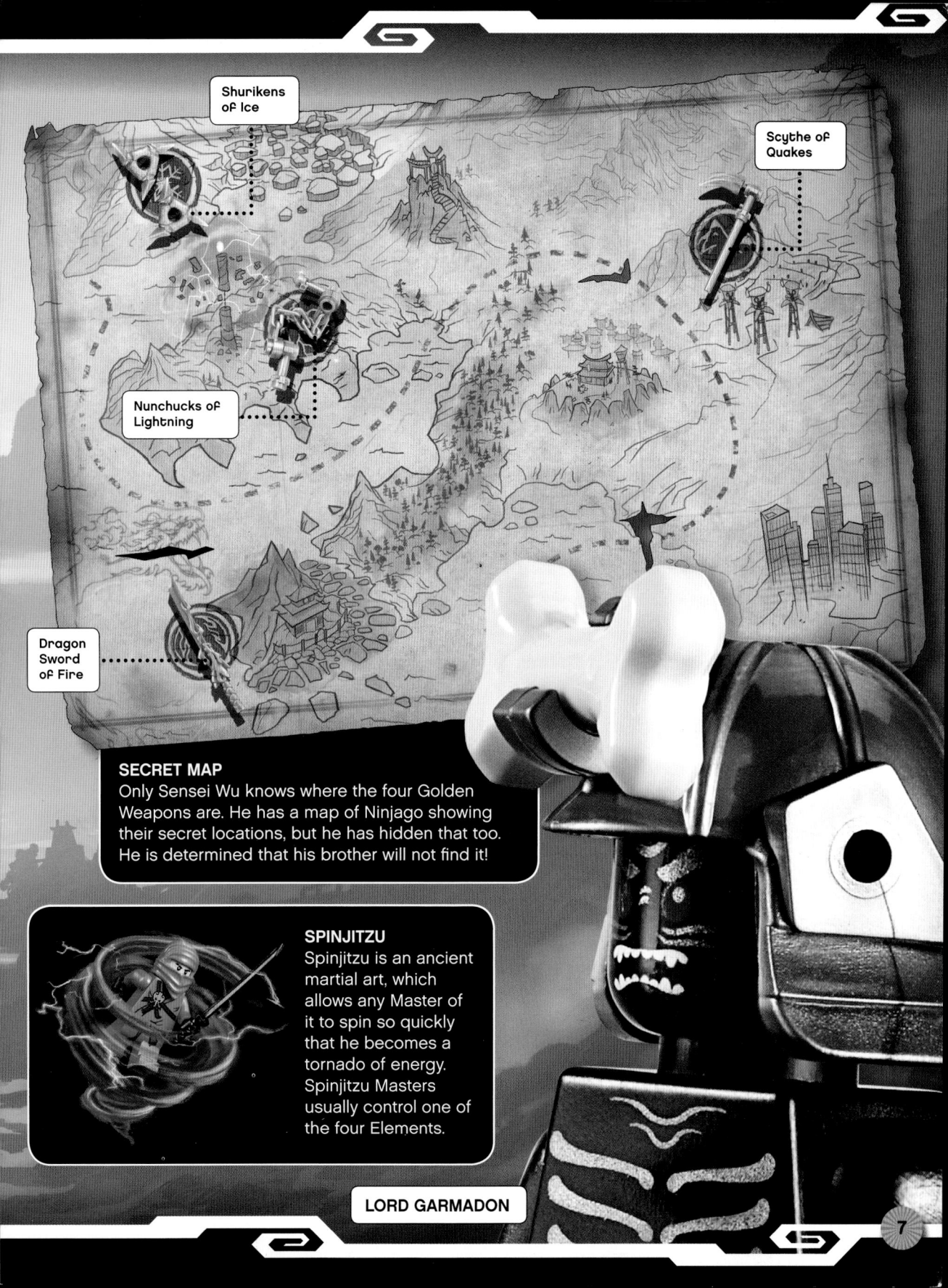

SECRET MAP
Only Sensei Wu knows where the four Golden Weapons are. He has a map of Ninjago showing their secret locations, but he has hidden that too. He is determined that his brother will not find it!

SPINJITZU
Spinjitzu is an ancient martial art, which allows any Master of it to spin so quickly that he becomes a tornado of energy. Spinjitzu Masters usually control one of the four Elements.

NINJA VS. SKELETON
I WILL NOT BE DEFEATED BY A PILE OF BONES! NINJA-GO!

SEASON ONE OF LEGO® Ninjago sees the return of Lord Garmadon. Sensei Wu trains four Ninja to help him defeat his evil brother. However, Garmadon is not alone—he has a mighty Skeleton Army. A total of sixteen awesome LEGO sets bring the season one characters, weapons, vehicles, and locations to life. Turn the page to find out more...
BANZAI! MY ICY POWER WILL SOON QUENCH YOUR FIRE, NINJA!

LORD GARMADON RETURNS

Peace in Ninjago is about to come to an end: Lord Garmadon has returned from the Underworld to search for the four Golden Weapons. And this time he has brought reinforcements—an evil Skeleton Army (also known as Skulkins).

Sensei Wu has a plan. He seeks out four young men—Cole, Jay, Kai, and Zane—whom he can train to become Ninja. These four Ninja will learn to be great warriors, and each will become a master of one of the Elements and a protector of one of the four Golden Weapons.

The Ninja are first put to the test when the Skeletons kidnap Kai's sister, Nya, and steal the map showing the location of the Golden Weapons. The boys put their training into action to rescue Nya and defeat the Skulkins. They also find the Sword of Fire. Further battles follow as the Ninja seek to gain all the Golden Weapons.

In one final attempt to beat his brother, Sensei Wu, Lord Garmadon lures the Ninja to his Dark Fortress. Can the Ninja defeat the mighty Lord Garmadon and his evil Skeleton Army? Turn to p.86 to find out!

FOUR BRAVE BOYS
Sensei Wu wants each of the Ninja to become a Spinjitzu Master of their Elements, so that they can help him prevent his evil brother, Lord Garmadon, from destroying Ninjago.

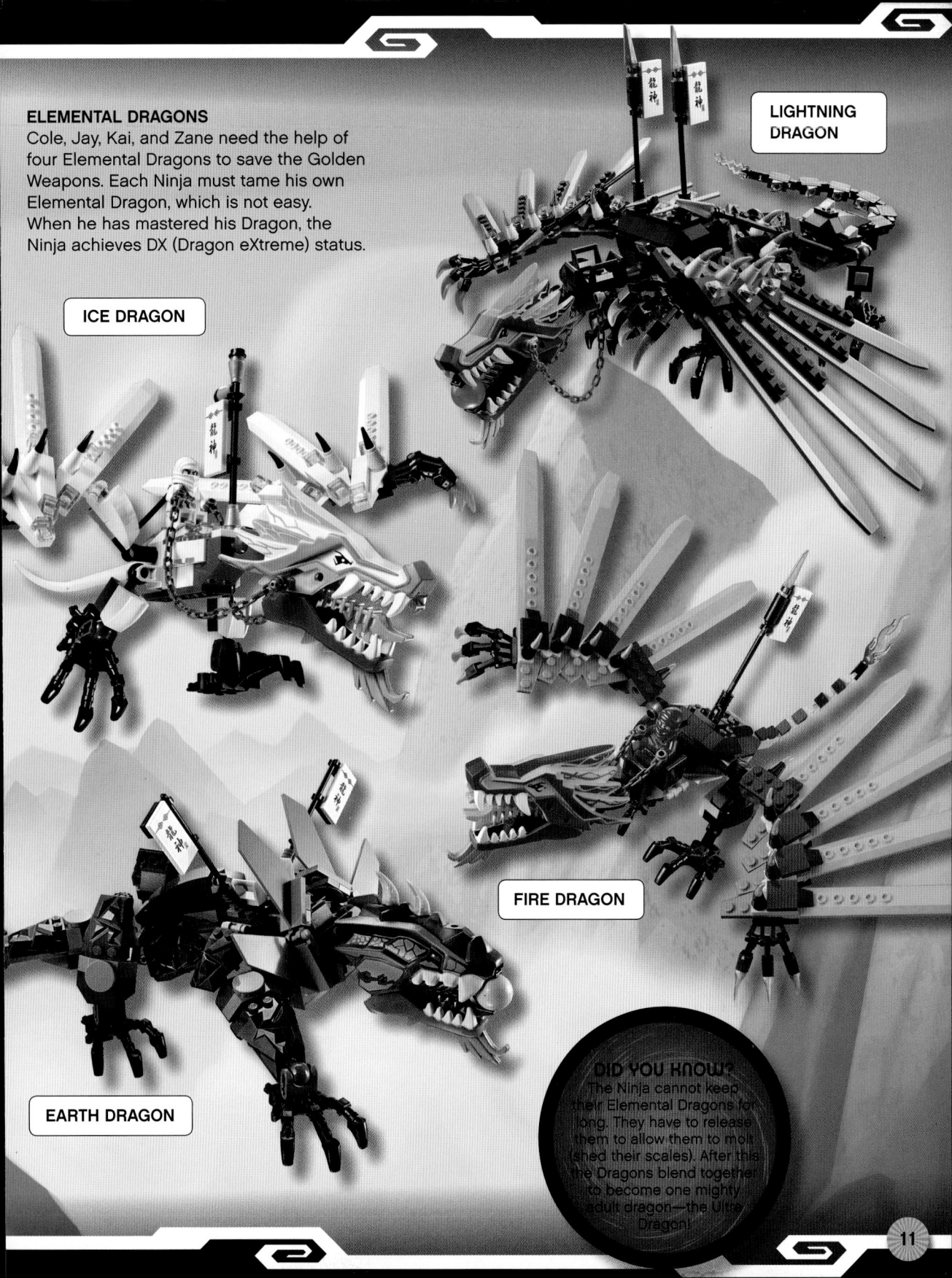
ELEMENTAL DRAGONS
Cole, Jay, Kai, and Zane need the help of four Elemental Dragons to save the Golden Weapons. Each Ninja must tame his own Elemental Dragon, which is not easy. When he has mastered his Dragon, the Ninja achieves DX (Dragon eXtreme) status.
LIGHTNING DRAGON
ICE DRAGON
FIRE DRAGON
EARTH DRAGON
DID YOU KNOW?
The Ninja cannot keep their Elemental Dragons for long. They have to release them to allow them to molt (shed their scales). After this the Dragons blend together to become one mighty adult dragon—the Ultra Dragon!

MEET THE NINJA

ALL THAT STANDS between Lord Garmadon and the four Golden Weapons is Sensei Wu and his four Ninja. Each individual Ninja is strong and brave, but together they are more than a match for the dark Lord and his Skeleton Army. Sensei Wu has trained them well. Young Nya longs to be a Ninja, like her brother, but she is not ready to join them yet.

SENSEI WU

Wise Sensei Wu knows what it takes to be a great Ninja, so he can see who has potential. He chooses four boys to help him save Ninjago from his brother.

KAI

Before he became a Ninja, Kai was a blacksmith. Now he is the Ninja of Fire!

ZANE

Ice Ninja Zane looks human but he is actually a robot. His fellow Ninja Jay calls him a "nindroid!"

NYA

Nya is Kai's younger sister. She also used to be a blacksmith, but now she wants to help save Ninjago.

JAY

Lightning Ninja Jay is as fast as Lightning, especially when he is doing Spinjitzu!

COLE

Earth Ninja Cole is the leader of the team, and the strongest. He is not to be messed with!

DO YOU HAVE THE SKILLS?

TO BECOME A TRUE NINJA YOU MUST:

FIND AND CONTROL YOUR ELEMENT

ALWAYS BE LOYAL TO YOUR FRIENDS

LEARN TO WIELD MANY TYPES OF WEAPONS

MASTER THE ART OF STEALTH

KAI

NINJA OF FIRE

THIS MINIFIGURE'S Element is Fire and his temper is hot! Kai accepts Sensei Wu's challenge to train as a Ninja, but he must work hard to control his anger and impatience. Sensei Wu's faith in Kai is justified—he becomes a brave, loyal, and skillful Ninja warrior.

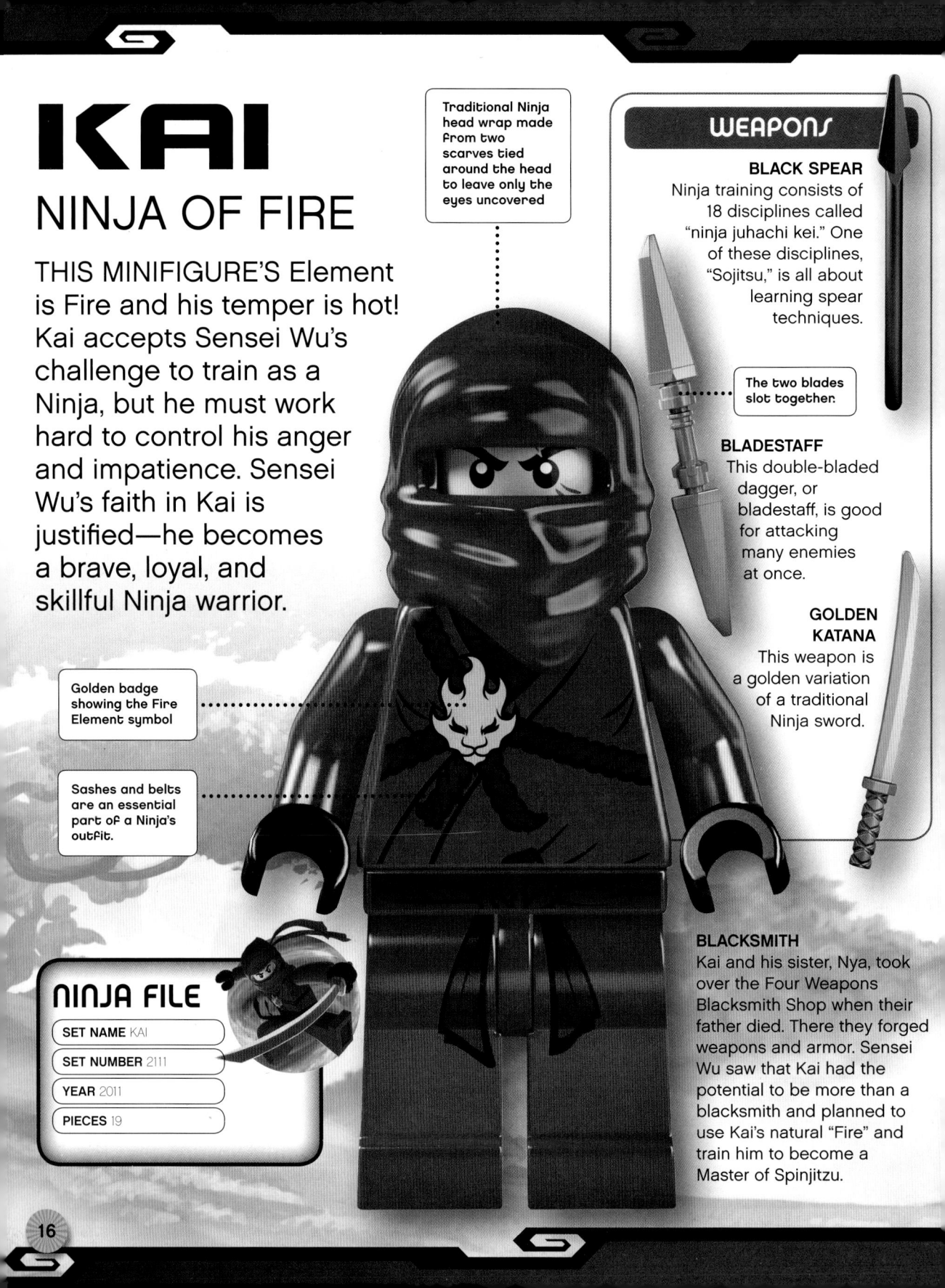

WEAPONS

BLACK SPEAR
Ninja training consists of 18 disciplines called "ninja juhachi kei." One of these disciplines, "Sojitsu," is all about learning spear techniques.

The two blades slot together.

BLADESTAFF
This double-bladed dagger, or bladestaff, is good for attacking many enemies at once.

GOLDEN KATANA
This weapon is a golden variation of a traditional Ninja sword.

NINJA FILE

SET NAME KAI
SET NUMBER 2111
YEAR 2011
PIECES 19

BLACKSMITH
Kai and his sister, Nya, took over the Four Weapons Blacksmith Shop when their father died. There they forged weapons and armor. Sensei Wu saw that Kai had the potential to be more than a blacksmith and planned to use Kai's natural "Fire" and train him to become a Master of Spinjitzu.

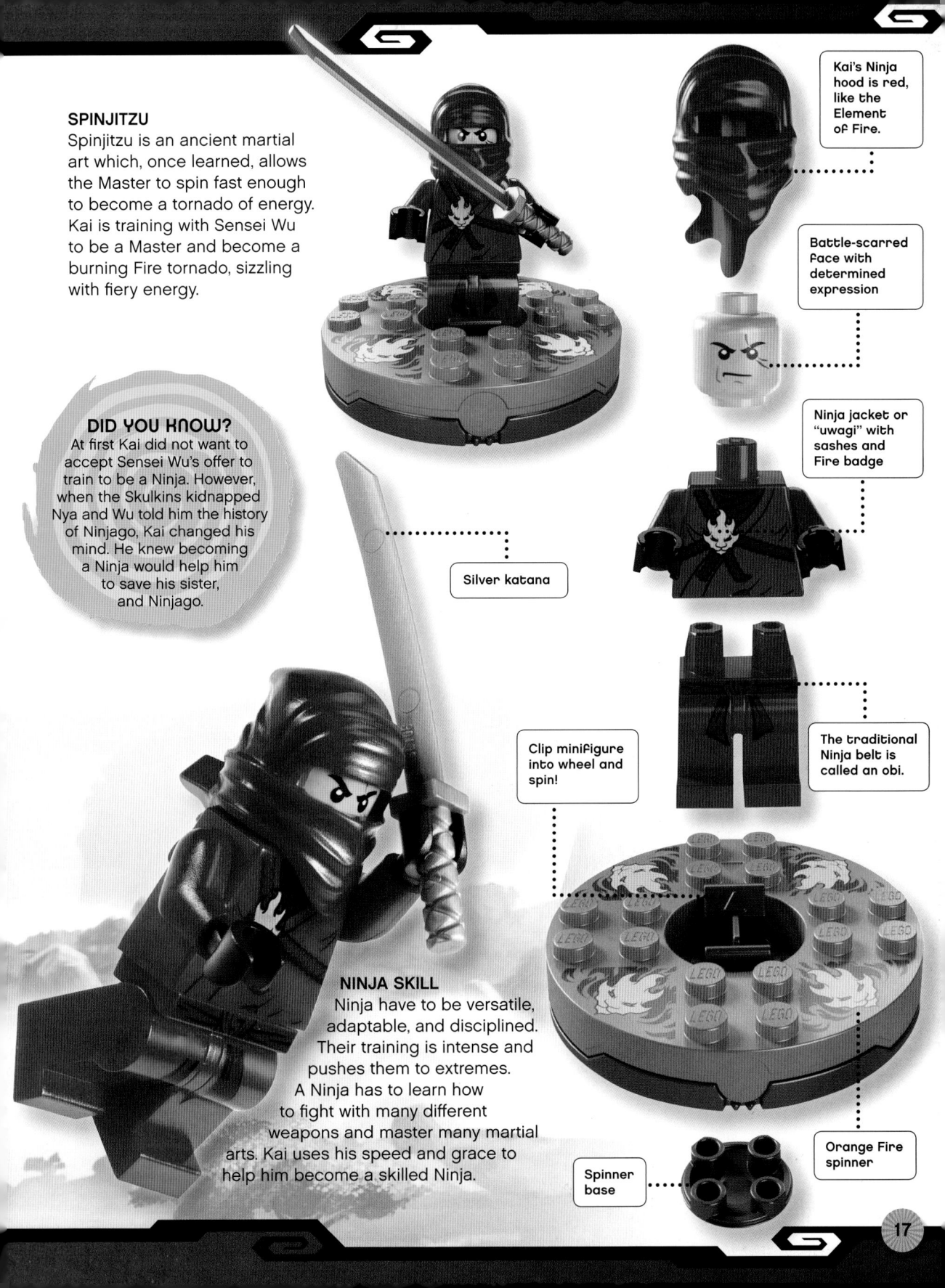

SPINJITZU

Spinjitzu is an ancient martial art which, once learned, allows the Master to spin fast enough to become a tornado of energy. Kai is training with Sensei Wu to be a Master and become a burning Fire tornado, sizzling with fiery energy.

DID YOU KNOW?

At first Kai did not want to accept Sensei Wu's offer to train to be a Ninja. However, when the Skulkins kidnapped Nya and Wu told him the history of Ninjago, Kai changed his mind. He knew becoming a Ninja would help him to save his sister, and Ninjago.

NINJA SKILL

Ninja have to be versatile, adaptable, and disciplined. Their training is intense and pushes them to extremes. A Ninja has to learn how to fight with many different weapons and master many martial arts. Kai uses his speed and grace to help him become a skilled Ninja.

NYA

SISTER OF FIRE

NYA IS KAI'S younger sister. She works with Kai in the Four Weapons Blacksmith Shop. Although she isn't a Ninja, Nya is determined to be better than the boys. She trains hard and, with a veil to mask her identity, she is always ready to battle evil.

NINJA FILE

SET NAME NYA

SET NUMBER 2172

YEAR 2011

PIECES 21

Red veil to hide her identity

Sleeveless red dress decorated with a phoenix bird pattern

WEAPONS

STAFF
This large wooden pole is a powerful defensive weapon, especially in the hands of a skilled fighter like Nya.

Sharp golden blade

GOLDEN NICK DAGGERS
The golden dagger is seriously sharp and especially effective when used in a pair.

GIRL POWER
Nya is kind and gentle, but also courageous and brave. She is gifted with natural psychic powers. All Nya's special abilities prove very useful when she is battling the evil Skeleton Army.

SECRET SPINNER

Nya hides her true identity so that she can help the Ninja in their fight against evil. With her super secret skills and her orange fire spinner, Nya can spin up a fiery tornado of energy. GO NYA, NINJA-GO!

DID YOU KNOW?
Nya and Lloyd Garmadon are the only two LEGO Ninjago minifigures to have double-sided heads.

SECRET CRUSH

When she is not battling Skeletons or Serpents, Nya wants to spend time with her favorite Ninja—Jay. Blue is Nya's favorite color so naturally Jay is her favorite Ninja!

BLACKSMITH SHOP

FAMILY BUSINESS

KAI AND NYA run their father's blacksmith shop, the Four Weapons. Their father was Sensei Wu's most trusted friend, so Wu asked him to draw a map showing the locations of the hiding place of the four Weapons of Spinjitzu. Kai and Nya's father hid the map inside the banner of the shop.

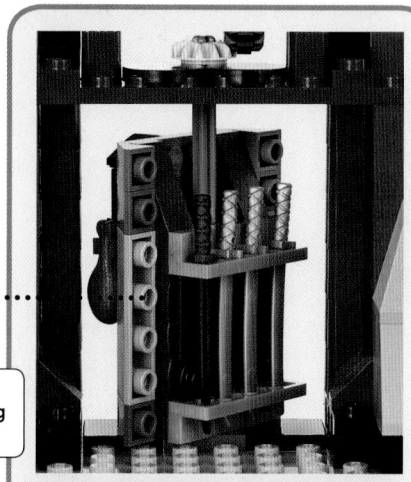

SECRET GEARS
When the roof is lifted it also uncovers a secret gear mechanism, which turns to reveal even more hidden weapons—four Ninja swords!

SECRET WEAPONS
Lift the roof of the shop to reveal a hidden rack on its underside that holds axes, spears, and other weapons and Ninja accessories.

Arsenal of weapons

Roof hinge and gear mechanism

Map shows the location of Golden Weapons

Weapons clip onto the underside of the roof

Golden katana sword on blacksmith's work bench

MINIFIGURES
Kruncha comes to the Four Weapons to steal the Golden Weapons secret location map. Kai has to fight him off using his hidden stash of weapons.

Kruncha

Kai

NINJA FILE

SET NAME BLACKSMITH SHOP

SET NUMBER 2508

YEAR 2011

PIECES 189

Lift hinged roof to reveal weapon rack and cog

Chimney

Water pool for cooling newly forged weapons

The other side of the secret spinning sword rack holds a hammer and a chicken leg.

SENSEI WU

SPINJITZU MASTER

MASTER OF THE power of creation, Sensei Wu is the son of the first Spinjitzu Master who created Ninjago. He is also the brother of Lord Garmadon. Sensei Wu is strong, wise, and patient. His mission is to protect Ninjago...

Traditional conical hat, often worn by farmers or monks

Sensei Wu's beard and mustache are removable.

Black kimono robe with golden writing to protect Sensei Wu from evil

NINJA FILE

SET NAME SENSEI WU

SET NUMBER 2255

YEAR 2011

PIECES 20

WEAPONS

STAFF OF THE DRAGONS
Spun quickly, the staff becomes a crushing wall with the strength of a dragon.

Tooth of a golden T-Rex

GOLDEN CHAINED FANG
This chained fang is one of the most valuable weapons in Ninjago.

GOLDEN KATANA
The katana is the most famous, expensive, and prized Japanese sword.

NINJA MASTER
Sensei Wu may be very old, but he is an expert Ninja and a fearless warrior. Wu makes his students train every day, and tells them to use their brains as well as their strength. Without wisdom you can't win.

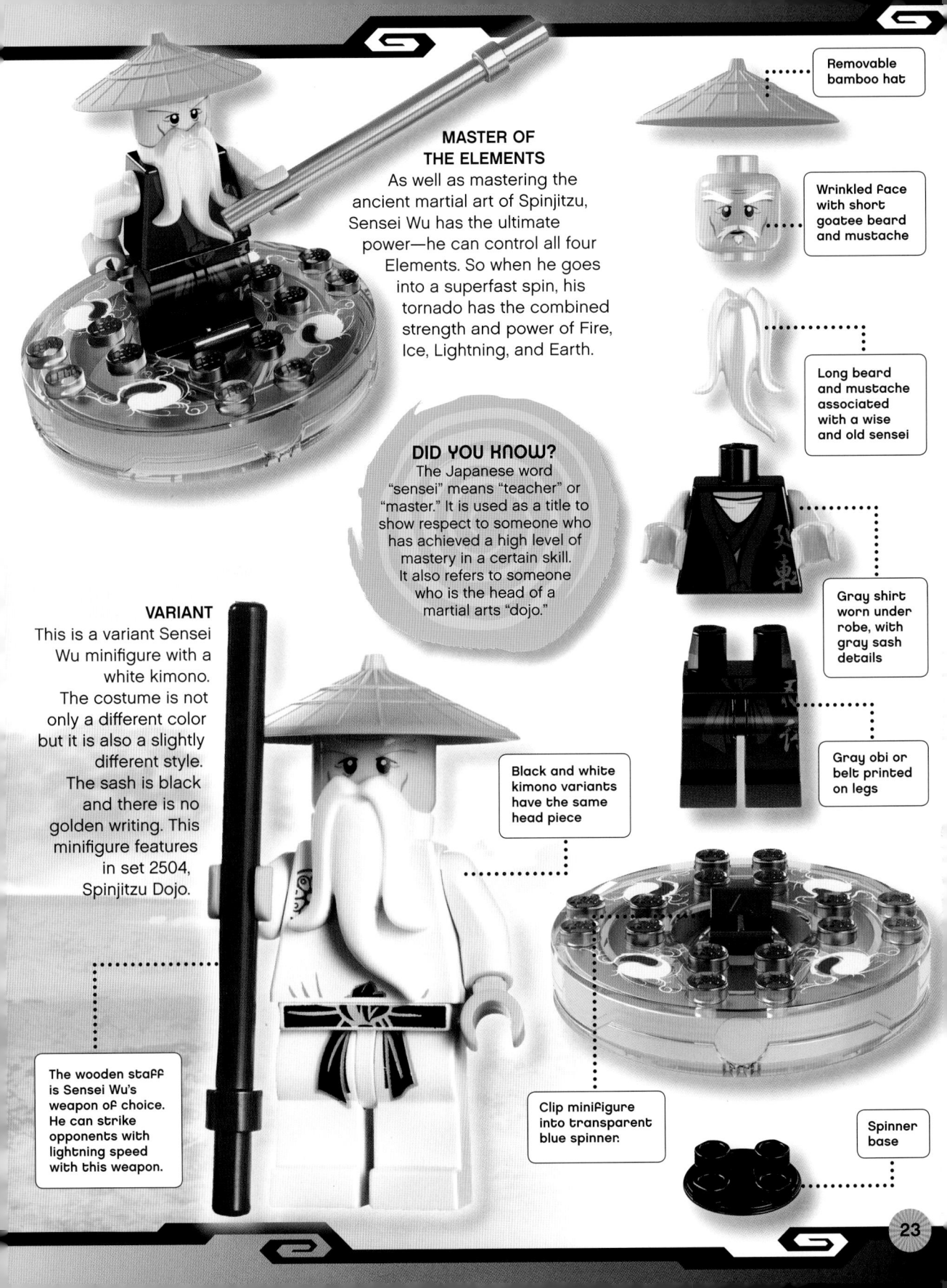

MASTER OF THE ELEMENTS

As well as mastering the ancient martial art of Spinjitzu, Sensei Wu has the ultimate power—he can control all four Elements. So when he goes into a superfast spin, his tornado has the combined strength and power of Fire, Ice, Lightning, and Earth.

DID YOU KNOW?

The Japanese word "sensei" means "teacher" or "master." It is used as a title to show respect to someone who has achieved a high level of mastery in a certain skill. It also refers to someone who is the head of a martial arts "dojo."

VARIANT

This is a variant Sensei Wu minifigure with a white kimono. The costume is not only a different color but it is also a slightly different style. The sash is black and there is no golden writing. This minifigure features in set 2504, Spinjitzu Dojo.

SPINJITZU DOJO

NINJA TRAINING

A DOJO IS a special place where the Ninja go to train. Sensei Wu makes the four Ninja work very hard—they have to dodge falling axes, avoid spinning swords, and swing over snake and fire pits. With practice, these challenges are no problem for the Ninja.

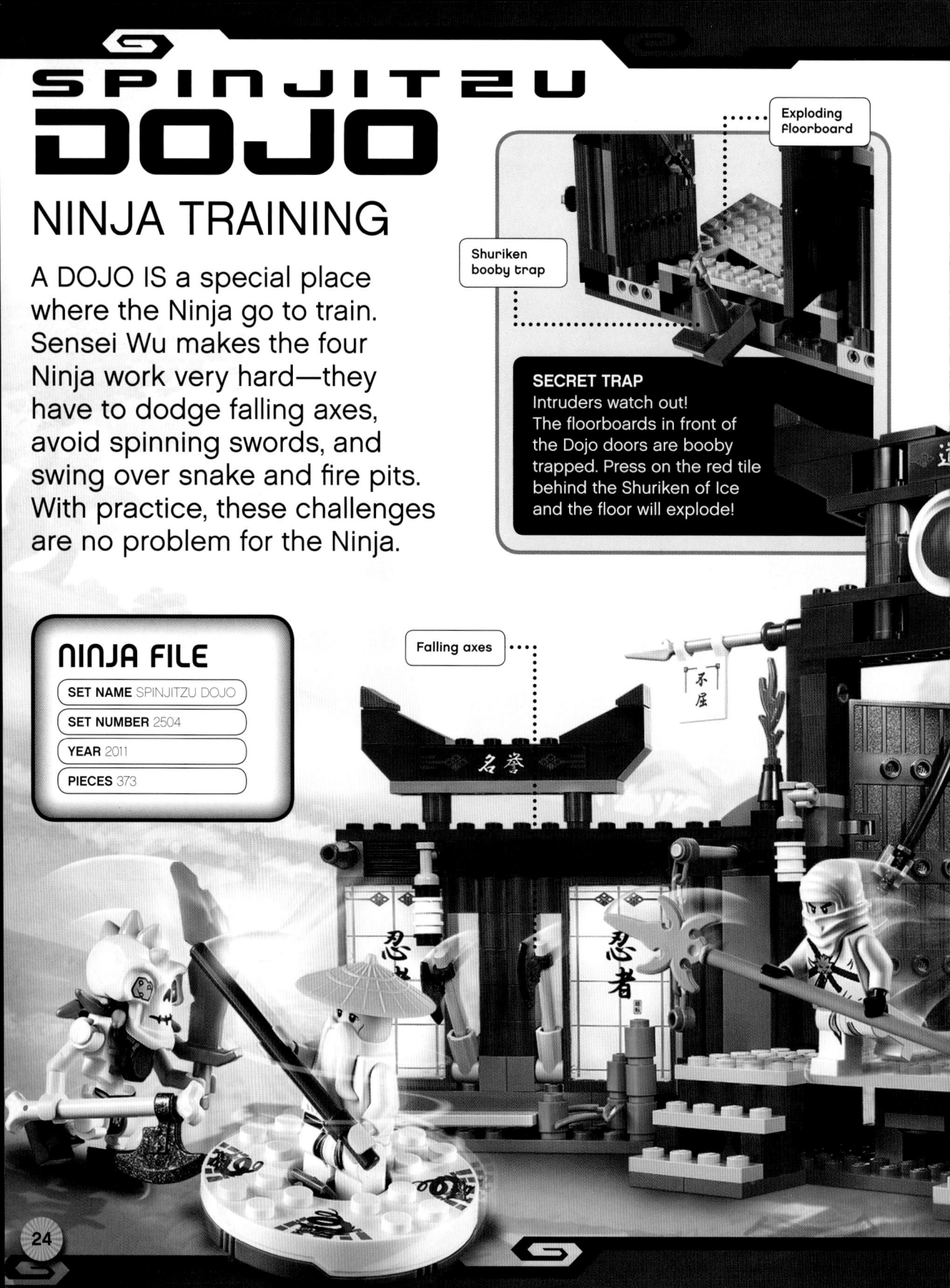

SECRET TRAP
Intruders watch out!
The floorboards in front of the Dojo doors are booby trapped. Press on the red tile behind the Shuriken of Ice and the floor will explode!

NINJA FILE

SET NAME SPINJITZU DOJO
SET NUMBER 2504
YEAR 2011
PIECES 373

MINIFIGURES
Can Zane prove that he has what it takes to be a Spinjitzu Master by stopping Nuckal from stealing the Shurikens of Ice?

DOJO ATTACK
One day, Sensei Wu is training Zane when General Nuckal attempts to steal the Shurikens of Ice. It's two Ninja versus one mean Skeleton. NINJA-GO!

SPINNING WEAPONS
Turn the small black wheel to spin the katanas. Zane must dodge the spinning swords as he walks along the narrow plank.

Doors open into the Dojo

Minifigures can walk on the wall by clipping their feet on here.

Shuriken of Ice mounted on a booby trap

Wall-mounted flick spear

Spinning swords

JAY

NINJA OF LIGHTNING

LIGHTNING IS HIS Element and Jay is lightning-fast in combat. His flair for crazy inventions, his thirst for adventure, and his sense of humor are just some of the qualities that Sensei Wu knew would make him a good skillful Ninja. Jay is also creative and loves solving problems.

NINJA FILE

SET NAME SPINJITZU STARTER SET

SET NUMBER 2257

YEAR 2011

PIECES 57

Traditional Ninja hood in blue, Jay's elemental color

NINJA TRAINING
Jay often uses his sense of humor to distract his enemies in battle, but he always takes his Ninja duties seriously. His lightning speed and agility mean he can easily wield two weapons at once to counter a double attack!

WEAPONS

SILVER KATANA
All Ninja must be able to fight with a sword. The training is tiring and difficult, but Ninja have to learn to persevere. Jay never gives up on anything.

GOLDEN SPEAR
The rarest of the Ninja spears, this golden weapon is extremely sharp and dangerous.

STAFF
Simple but effective, this basic Ninja weapon is useful in one-on-one combat.

Golden emblem on robe is the symbol for Lightning

The Ninja sash is a good place to hide weapons.

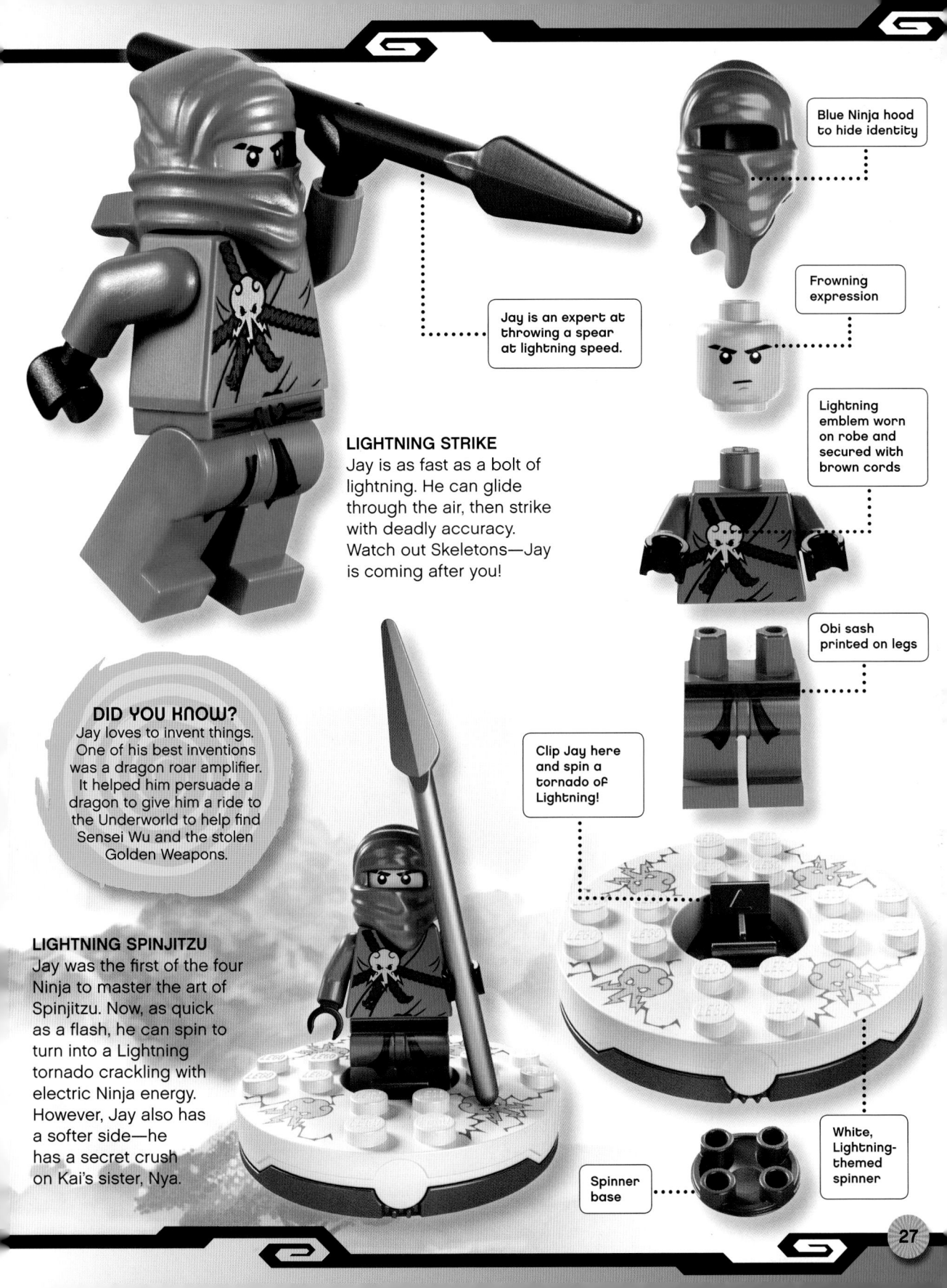

LIGHTNING STRIKE
Jay is as fast as a bolt of lightning. He can glide through the air, then strike with deadly accuracy. Watch out Skeletons—Jay is coming after you!

DID YOU KNOW?
Jay loves to invent things. One of his best inventions was a dragon roar amplifier. It helped him persuade a dragon to give him a ride to the Underworld to help find Sensei Wu and the stolen Golden Weapons.

LIGHTNING SPINJITZU
Jay was the first of the four Ninja to master the art of Spinjitzu. Now, as quick as a flash, he can spin to turn into a Lightning tornado crackling with electric Ninja energy. However, Jay also has a softer side—he has a secret crush on Kai's sister, Nya.

COLE

NINJA OF EARTH

JUST LIKE EARTH, his Element, Cole is as strong and reliable as a rock. Cole's natural strategic and leadership skills make him a key part of the team. Cole always puts his team first and is a true friend to the other Ninja.

WEAPONS

BLACK KATANA
To be a skilled swordsman, training is essential. The katana is not an easy weapon to master.

STAFF OF THE DRAGONS
In the hands of a Spinjitzu Master, this Golden Staff will knock the enemy out cold.

HAMMER
This is a good weapon for a fight with a Skeleton!

A Ninja wrap provides a good disguise.

Golden emblem showing the Earth symbol

An obi is a good place to hide weapons.

NINJA FILE

SET NAME COLE
SET NUMBER 2112
YEAR 2011
PIECES 19

TEAM FIRST
Cole lacked direction and purpose when he first met Sensei Wu. However, becoming a Ninja has changed him. Now Cole enjoys helping others. A successful mission makes him happy and he always puts his team first, whatever the risks to himself.

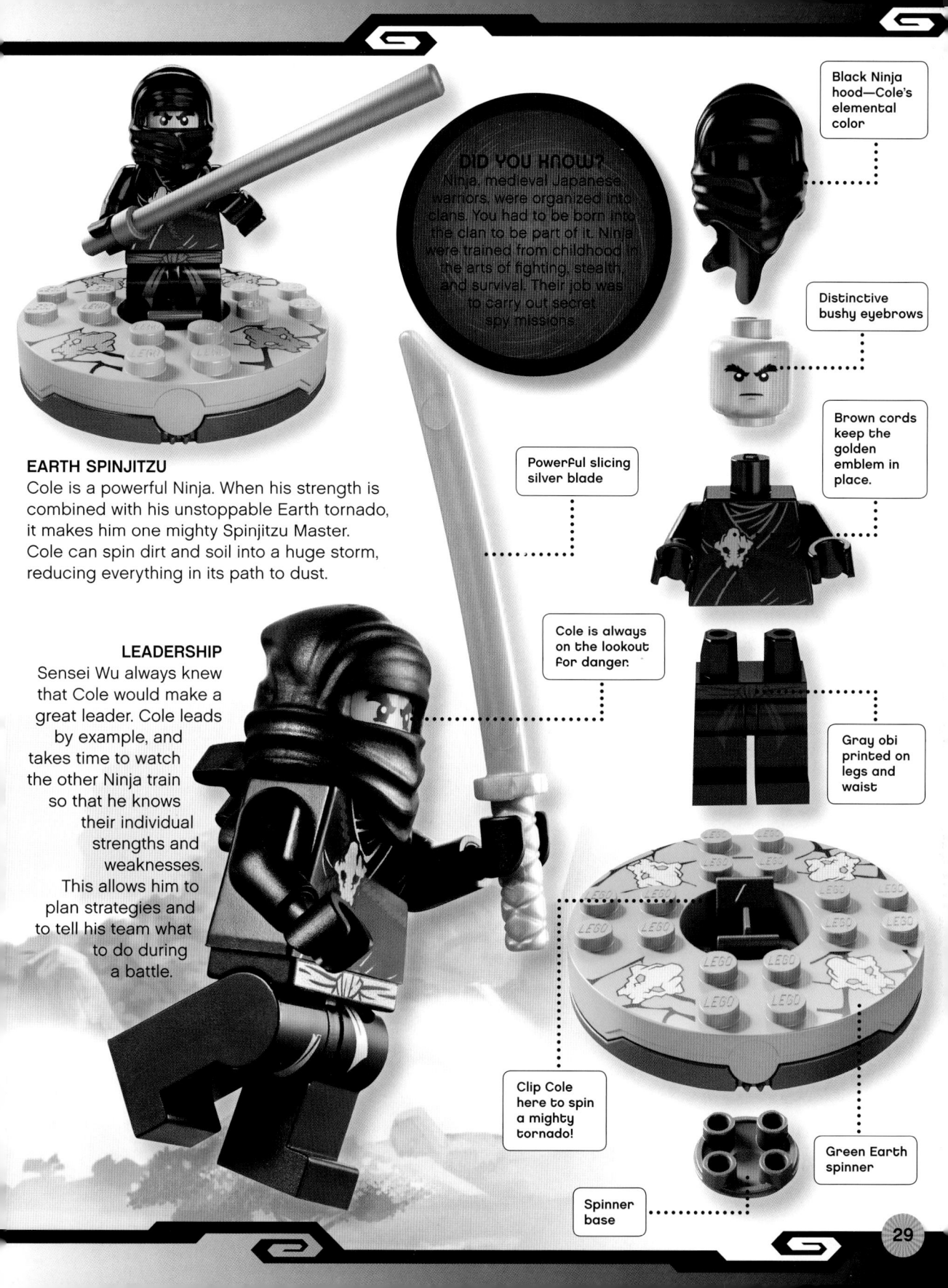

DID YOU KNOW?
Ninja, medieval Japanese warriors, were organized into clans. You had to be born into the clan to be part of it. Ninja were trained from childhood in the arts of fighting, stealth, and survival. Their job was to carry out secret spy missions.

EARTH SPINJITZU
Cole is a powerful Ninja. When his strength is combined with his unstoppable Earth tornado, it makes him one mighty Spinjitzu Master. Cole can spin dirt and soil into a huge storm, reducing everything in its path to dust.

LEADERSHIP
Sensei Wu always knew that Cole would make a great leader. Cole leads by example, and takes time to watch the other Ninja train so that he knows their individual strengths and weaknesses. This allows him to plan strategies and to tell his team what to do during a battle.

ZANE

NINJA OF ICE

ZANE IS QUIET, serious, and focused. He learns quickly and is curious about everything. Zane is a seer with the power of sixth sense, and it makes him a particularly stealthy warrior. However, Zane has a forgotten past that sets him apart from the other Ninja.

NINJA FILE

SET NAME ZANE

SET NUMBER 2113

YEAR 2011

PIECES 19

Zane's Ninja wrap is as icy white as his Element.

Golden emblem to represent Element of Ice

Traditional Ninja sash belt to hold robe in place

WEAPONS

FLAT SPEAR
In the hands of a trained Ninja, the spear is a lethal weapon of deadly accuracy.

SILVER KATANA
This prized sword is a top Ninja weapon.

SHURIKENS OF ICE
One of the four Golden Weapons, these icy throwing stars slice through the air to hit their target with force.

NINJA SKILLS
Zane watches and waits for the right moment to strike! He is so quiet and stealthy that he can creep up on his enemies without being detected. He is dedicated and precise in combat, and ready to tackle any task.

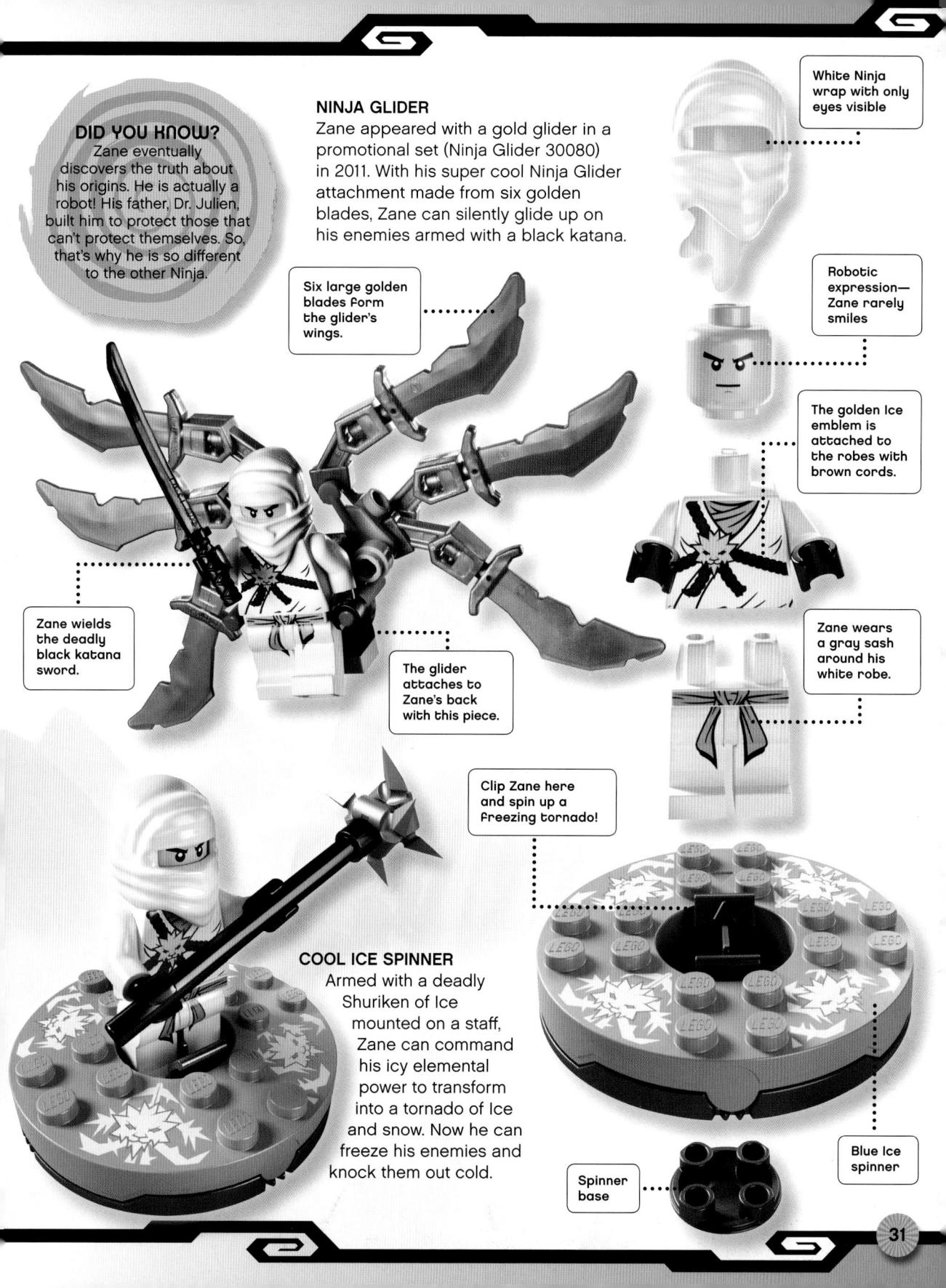

DID YOU KNOW?

Zane eventually discovers the truth about his origins. He is actually a robot! His father, Dr. Julien, built him to protect those that can't protect themselves. So, that's why he is so different to the other Ninja.

NINJA GLIDER

Zane appeared with a gold glider in a promotional set (Ninja Glider 30080) in 2011. With his super cool Ninja Glider attachment made from six golden blades, Zane can silently glide up on his enemies armed with a black katana.

COOL ICE SPINNER

Armed with a deadly Shuriken of Ice mounted on a staff, Zane can command his icy elemental power to transform into a tornado of Ice and snow. Now he can freeze his enemies and knock them out cold.

MOUNTAIN SHRINE

SECRET TRAINING GROUND

KAI IS TRAINING hard at the secret Mountain Shrine to increase his Dragon eXtreme (DX) power and master the next level of Spinjitzu. He will need all his skills to protect the Dragon Sword of Fire and his treasure from the evil Skeleton Army.

NINJA FILE

SET NAME MOUNTAIN SHRINE

SET NUMBER 2254

YEAR 2011

PIECES 169

TARGET PRACTICE

The Mountain Shrine set features lots of different weapons and equipment—a double scythe, a chain, a spiked mace ball, and a punching bag. However, Kai's most prized weapon is the rare and precious Golden Dragon Sword!

HIDDEN TREASURE

This set features a treasure chest which can be hidden in the arch underneath the shrine and pulled out when the arch rotates. It also includes a skeleton-style dummy for target practice.

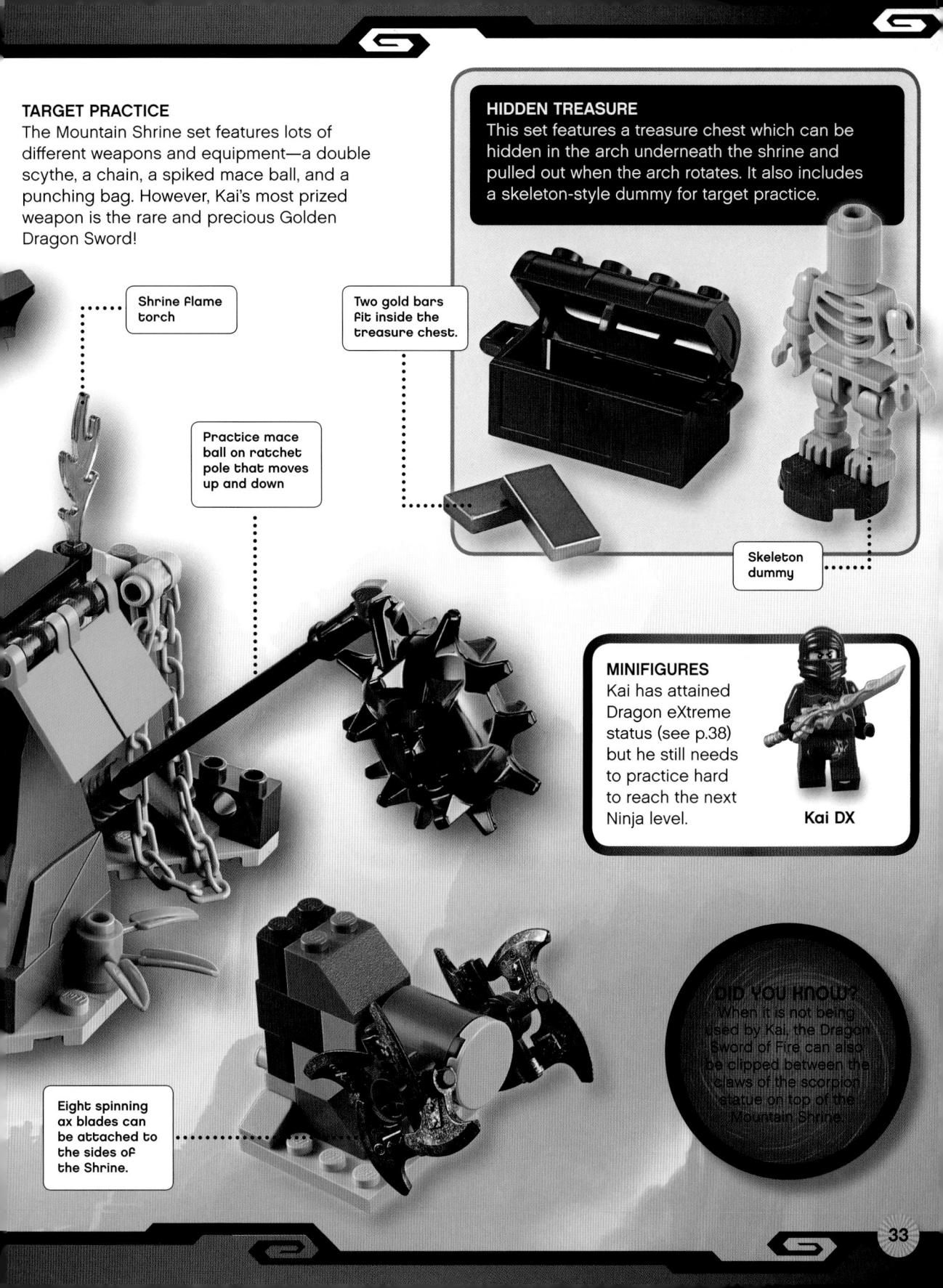

MINIFIGURES

Kai has attained Dragon eXtreme status (see p.38) but he still needs to practice hard to reach the next Ninja level.

Kai DX

DID YOU KNOW?

When it is not being used by Kai, the Dragon Sword of Fire can also be clipped between the claws of the scorpion statue on top of the Mountain Shrine.

TRAINING OUTPOST

ART OF SPINJITZU

THIS WEAPONS RACK is Cole's portable training outpost. He can set it up anytime and anywhere to practice his Spinjitzu skills. This set comes with five weapons—including two bowie knives—and an archery target.

NINJA FILE

SET NAME NINJA TRAINING OUTPOST
SET NUMBER 2516
YEAR 2011
PIECES 45

TARGET PRACTICE
Bullseye! A Ninja needs to have a deadly aim so Kai practices his shooting by firing arrows and throwing the knives at the target. The Skeleton Army had better watch out!

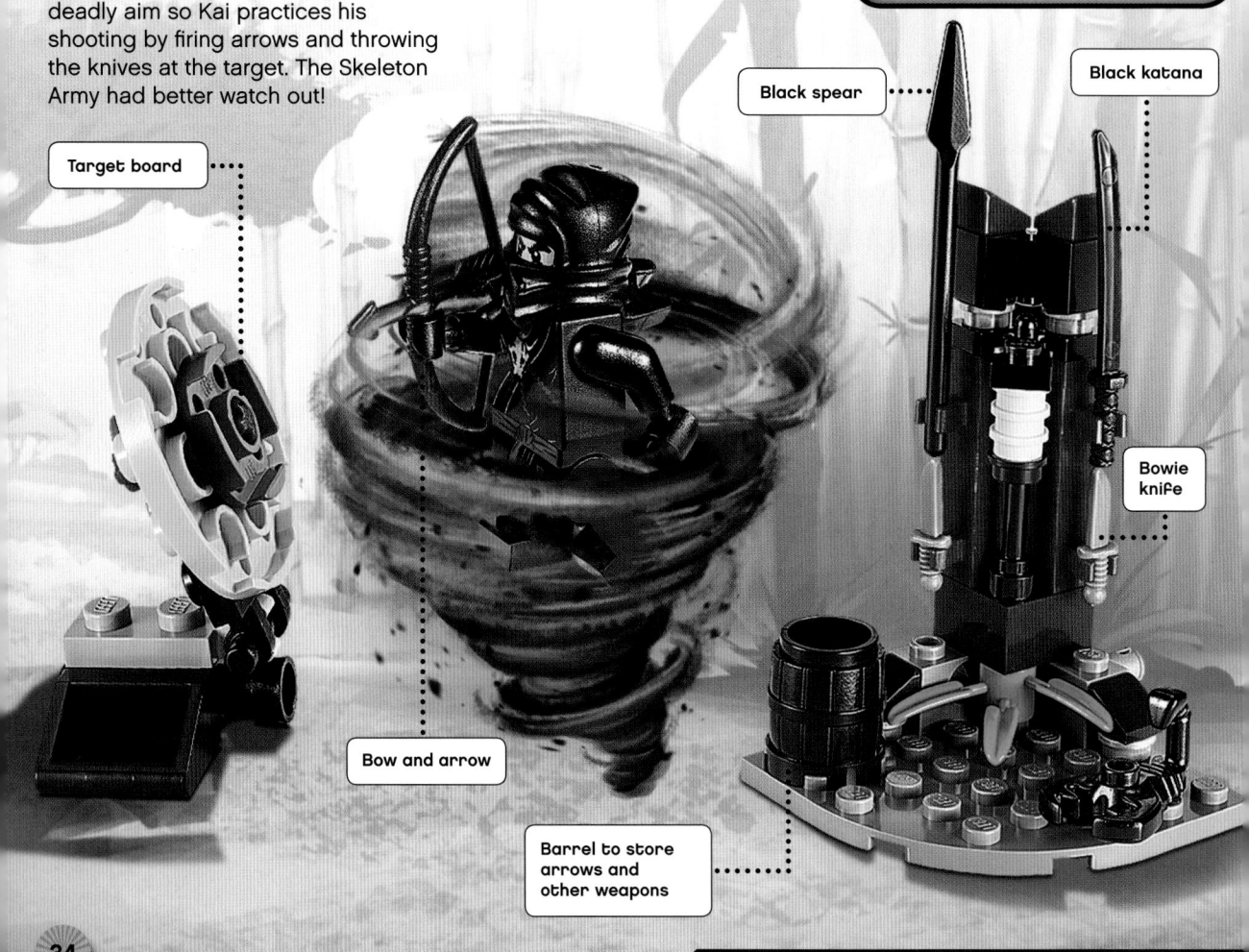

AMBUSH SHRINE

SKELETON ATTACK

SENSEI WU SENDS Kai into a bamboo forest to protect the Scythe of Quakes. But Bonezai wants the weapon too! Kai must hide among the trees and then launch himself at the bony villain. Kai will need his Ninja stealth to beat Bonezai.

NINJA FILE

SET NAME NINJA AMBUSH

SET NUMBER 2258

YEAR 2011

PIECES 71

FLYING ATTACK!
Flick the red LEGO piece down hard to launch the Ninja into the air from his hiding place behind the bamboo trees. NINJA-GO!

SPECTACULAR SET

The Fire Temple set is made up of five parts—the Fire Dragon, the two pretty side bridges, a front staircase, and the ornate main temple. Best of all, the Dragon can be fully detached from the Fire Temple.

FIRE TEMPLE

SECRET HIDING PLACE

SENSEI WU HAS hidden the Dragon Sword of Fire in the Fire Temple to stop his evil brother getting hold of it. Unfortunately, Lord Garmadon has discovered its location...

DRAGON OF FIRE
Pull the Dragon Sword of Fire to open up the Fire Temple. When the Temple is opened it reveals the Fire Dragon's hiding place. Beware any Skeletons who dare to enter...

Sword of Fire can be pulled here

Fire Dragon can launch balls of fire!

Garden shrine with gong and drum sticks

Cherry blossom tree and bridge

MINIFIGURES
This is the largest set in the first season of LEGO Ninjago. It has seven minifigures and includes all four Golden Weapons.

Zane

Sensei Wu

Samukai

Nya

Kai

Kruncha

Garmadon

NINJA FILE

SET NAME FIRE TEMPLE
SET NUMBER 2507
YEAR 2011
PIECES 1180

KAI DX

FIRE DRAGON EXTREME

KAI HAS MANAGED to tame his Dragon and has gained DX (Dragon eXtreme) ranking. This status is reflected in his minifigure's new Ninja Dragon costume. Kai received this robe after he had tamed his Dragon and found the Sword of Fire.

DX SPINNER
When a Ninja reaches DX ranking, his minifigure gets a super gold Spinjitzu spinner. Kai's DX spinner shows the Fire Element symbol. He can whip up a fiery tornado, which has the power and strength of a Dragon.

NINJA FILE

SET NAME FIRE TEMPLE
SET NUMBER 2507
YEAR 2011
PIECES 1180

Golden Fire Dragon printed on the robe breathes the Element of Fire

WEAPONS

Blade shoots fire balls

DRAGON SWORD OF FIRE
This powerful weapon can only be held by someone who has mastered Fire.

New dark red obi sash

DRAGON TAMER
Kai was the first of the Ninja to tame his Dragon. The Ninja needed the Dragons to take them to the Underworld to help Sensei Wu. Kai explained to the Dragon what he wanted and the Dragon agreed to help him.

FIRE DRAGON

FIRE GUARDIAN

THIS MIGHTY FIRE Dragon guards the Golden Dragon Sword of Fire, which Sensei Wu hid in the Fire Temple. When Kai tames this Dragon, he is able to control him.

NINJA FILE

SET NAME FIRE TEMPLE
SET NUMBER 2507
YEAR 2011
PIECES 1180

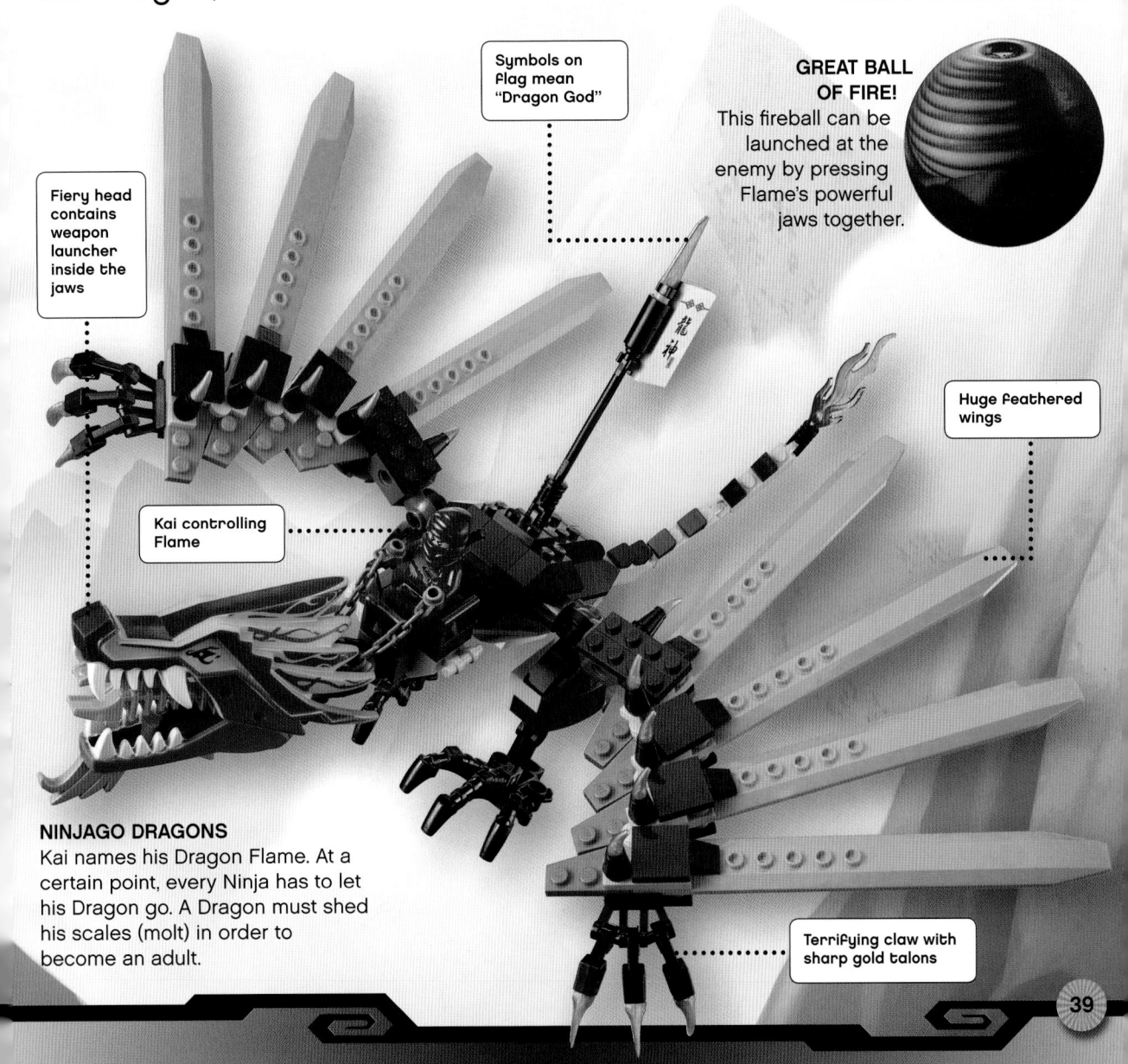

GREAT BALL OF FIRE!
This fireball can be launched at the enemy by pressing Flame's powerful jaws together.

NINJAGO DRAGONS
Kai names his Dragon Flame. At a certain point, every Ninja has to let his Dragon go. A Dragon must shed his scales (molt) in order to become an adult.

JAY DX

DRAGON EXTREME

JAY USED HIS inventing skills to tame his Dragon when his jokes and cooking failed to win the Dragon over (see p.27). With his DX Ninja status and the Nunchucks of Lightning, Jay is more than ready to battle against evil.

DX SPINNER
Jay's gold and gray DX spinner shows the Lightning Element symbol. In a flash, Jay spins up a real storm. He is a powerful force of nature ready to battle any enemy.

Golden Lightning Dragon printed on robe is breathing the Element of Lightning

WEAPONS

Curved, slender single-edged blade

BLACK KATANA
After a lot of training and practice, Jay can strike with the speed of lightning using his Ninja sword.

Lightning Dragon detail printed on legs

NINJA FILE

SET NAME LIGHTNING DRAGON BATTLE

SET NUMBER 2521

YEAR 2011

PIECES 645

THE NINJA LIFE
Being a Ninja is not just a job, it is a way of life. Every Ninja has to follow a special code of conduct and commit to the rigorous training and learning of new skills. Jay is a very dedicated Ninja.

LIGHTNING DRAGON

LIGHTNING GUARDIAN

THIS LIGHTNING DRAGON guards the Golden Nunchucks of Lightning, which Sensei Wu hid in the desolate Floating Ruins. Jay names his Dragon Wisp and once tamed, Wisp is forever loyal to Jay.

NINJA FILE

SET NAME LIGHTNING DRAGON BATTLE

SET NUMBER 2521

YEAR 2011

PIECES 645

BLUE LIGHTNING BALL
Press on the terrifying jaws to launch a lethal Lightning ball at lightning speed!

MYSTICAL BEASTS
Japanese dragons are known as "tatsu" or "ryu." They are serpent-like and have three-clawed feet. Black dragons symbolize the North; blue the East; white the South, and red the West.

COLE DX

EARTH DRAGON EXTREME

COLE HAS TO overcome his biggest fear—Dragons—to achieve his DX Ninja status. With the courage of a true leader, Cole conquers his fear and learns how to control his Dragon. He becomes very fond of the powerful beast.

DRAGON SPINNER
With the newly acquired skills of the Dragon Ninja, Cole can spin up an even bigger tornado. Combined with the power of the Scythe of Quakes, Cole is unstoppable!

NINJA FILE

SET NAME Cole DX
SET NUMBER 2170
YEAR 2011
PIECES 21

Golden Earth Dragon is breathing out the Element of Earth

WEAPONS

SILVER KATANA
Classic Ninja combat weapon.

BLACK SPEAR
A fast and accurate weapon in the hands of a Ninja.

SCYTHE OF QUAKES
This weapon can cause earthquakes with one mighty blow. It is the ultimate Serpentine repellent.

Earth Dragon's huge scaly tail printed on the legs

DETERMINATION
Cole takes his role as leader of the team very seriously. Now he has reached DX status, he won't rest until he has achieved the next Ninja level.

EARTH DRAGON

EARTH GUARDIAN

THIS AWESOME EARTH Dragon guards the Scythe of Quakes, which Sensei Wu hid in the Caves of Despair. He is the first of the four Elemental Dragons that the Ninja team encounter in their search for the Golden Weapons. As soon as Cole learns to control the Earth Dragon, he names him Rocky.

NINJA FILE

SET NAME EARTH DRAGON DEFENSE

SET NUMBER 2509

YEAR 2011

PIECES 227

STONE MISSILES
Press on the mighty jaws of this huge beast to fire stone ball missiles. The enemy will be falling like boulders!

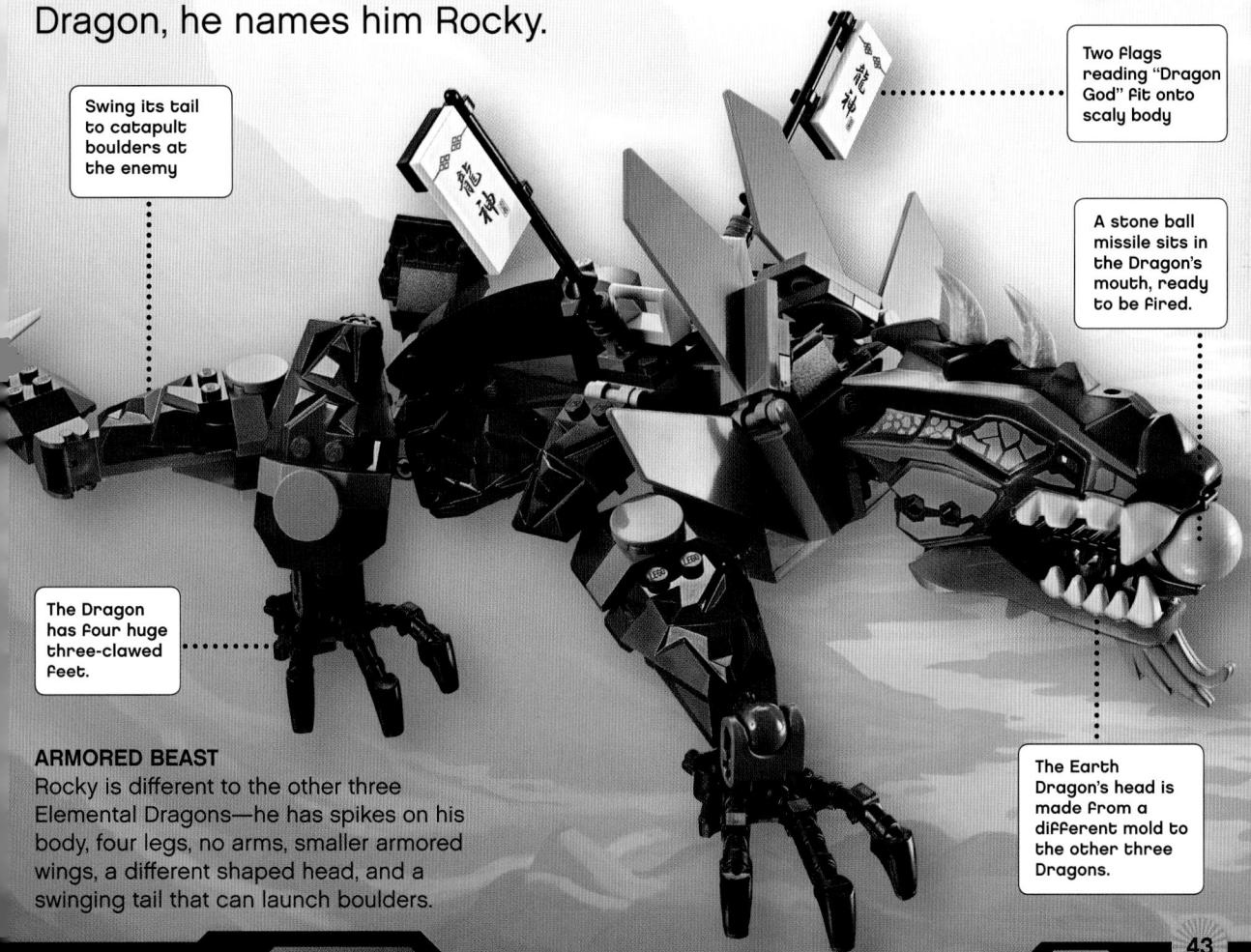

ARMORED BEAST
Rocky is different to the other three Elemental Dragons—he has spikes on his body, four legs, no arms, smaller armored wings, a different shaped head, and a swinging tail that can launch boulders.

ZANE DX

ICE DRAGON EXTREME

ZANE'S FIRST MEETING with his Dragon didn't go very well—the beast froze Zane into a solid block of ice! As soon as he had thawed out, Zane was able to tame the Dragon and earn his DX (Dragon eXtreme) Ninja status.

Removable hood

DRAGON SPINNER
As a DX Ninja, Zane has reached a higher level of Spinjitzu ability and can spin up a terrifying tornado of Ice and snow. Skulkins had better watch out!

NINJA FILE

SET NAME ZANE DX
SET NUMBER 2171
YEAR 2011
PIECES 22

Golden Ice Dragon breathes out the Element of Ice

WEAPONS

NINJAGO SWORD
Zane can wield this Ninja sword with great skill.

FLAIL OF ICE
This golden weapon has the power of solid Ice.

SILVER SPEAR
This weapon can be thrown at enemies.

Unique DX printing on torso and legs also continues on back of minifigure

ICE ATTACK!
Now that Zane is a Dragon Ninja, he plans to crush the Skeleton Army with a freezing Ice attack. With the help of his Dragon, Zane will be unstoppable!

ICE DRAGON

ICE GUARDIAN

THIS ICE DRAGON guards the Golden Shurikens of Ice, which Sensei Wu hid inside the Ice Fortress in the Frozen Wasteland. Zane uses his elemental powers to find a cool connection with the mythical beast. He tames the Dragon and names him Shard.

FROZEN BALLS OF ICE
Solid frozen Ice balls can be fired at speed from this icy beast's terrifying jaws.

Zane rides his Dragon from a seat on its back.

Ice feathered wings are movable

Terrifying orange claws

FROZEN BREATH
The Ice Dragon may be the smallest of the Elemental Dragons, but he is just as terrifying as the others. Icy breath shoots out from his jaws, freezing everything in its path.

Ice balls can be fired from the Dragon's jaws.

NINJA FILE

SET NAME ICE DRAGON ATTACK
SET NUMBER 2260
YEAR 2011
PIECES 158

MEET THE SKELETON ARMY

THE SKELETON ARMY is a scary sight to behold! These bony bad guys, also known as Skulkins, have come from the Underworld to create trouble in Ninjago. There are four Skulkin Generals and four soldiers. Some of the Skeletons are a little stupid and some are very smart, but all of them are determined to fight the Ninja!

LORD GARMADON

Lord Garmadon controls the Skeleton Army and it carries out his evil bidding.

SAMUKAI

Leader of the Skulkins and General of Fire, Samukai is often frustrated by the stupidity of his troops.

KRUNCHA

General Kruncha is Samukai's second-in-command. This fearsome Skulkin is famous for his strength.

WYPLASH

General Wyplash is one of the smartest Skeletons. He is good at thinking up nasty plans to thwart the Ninja.

NUCKAL

General Nuckal is very stupid. His contributions to the army include getting into trouble and irritating Kruncha.

BONEZAI

Bonezai is chief designer of all the Skeleton Army's vehicles, including helicopters, motorbikes, and trucks.

KRAZI

Don't be fooled by this wacky warrior, he's no joker. Krazi's speed on the battlefield is legendary.

FRAKJAW

Part of the attack unit, Frakjaw terrifies his enemies with his spiky weapon, also known as a silver battle mace.

CHOPOV

Chopov is famous for his defensive skills. The bony Skulkin also acts as the Skeleton Army's vehicle mechanic.

I'VE GOT A BONE TO PICK WITH THOSE NINJA!

THE BACKBONE OF THE SKELETON ARMY IS:

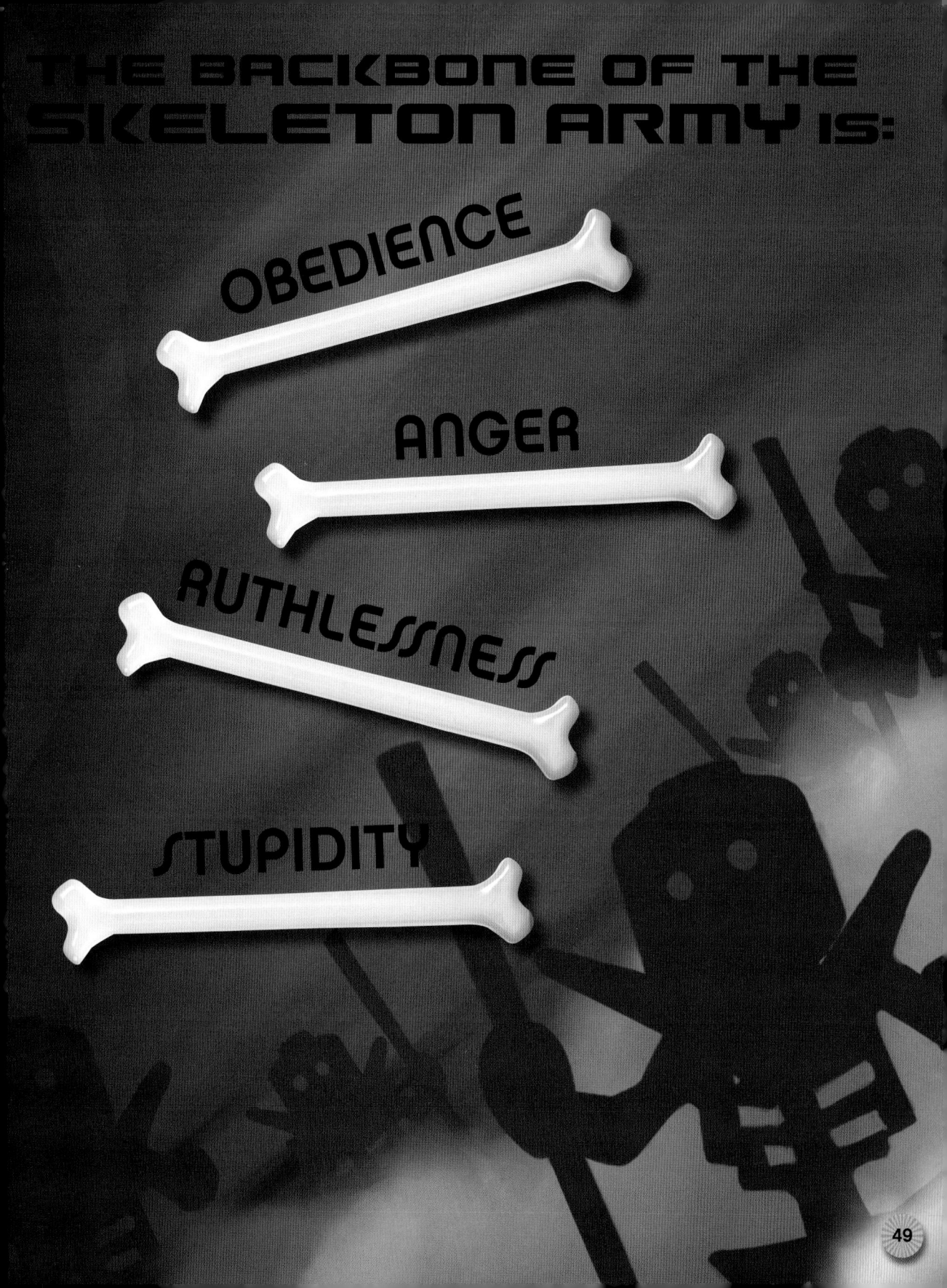

LORD GARMADON

MASTER OF DESTRUCTION

SENSEI WU'S EVIL brother Lord Garmadon is King of the Underworld. With the help of his Skeleton Army, he continues to spread fear on his dark quest to defeat his brother and the Ninja, and to destroy Ninjago.

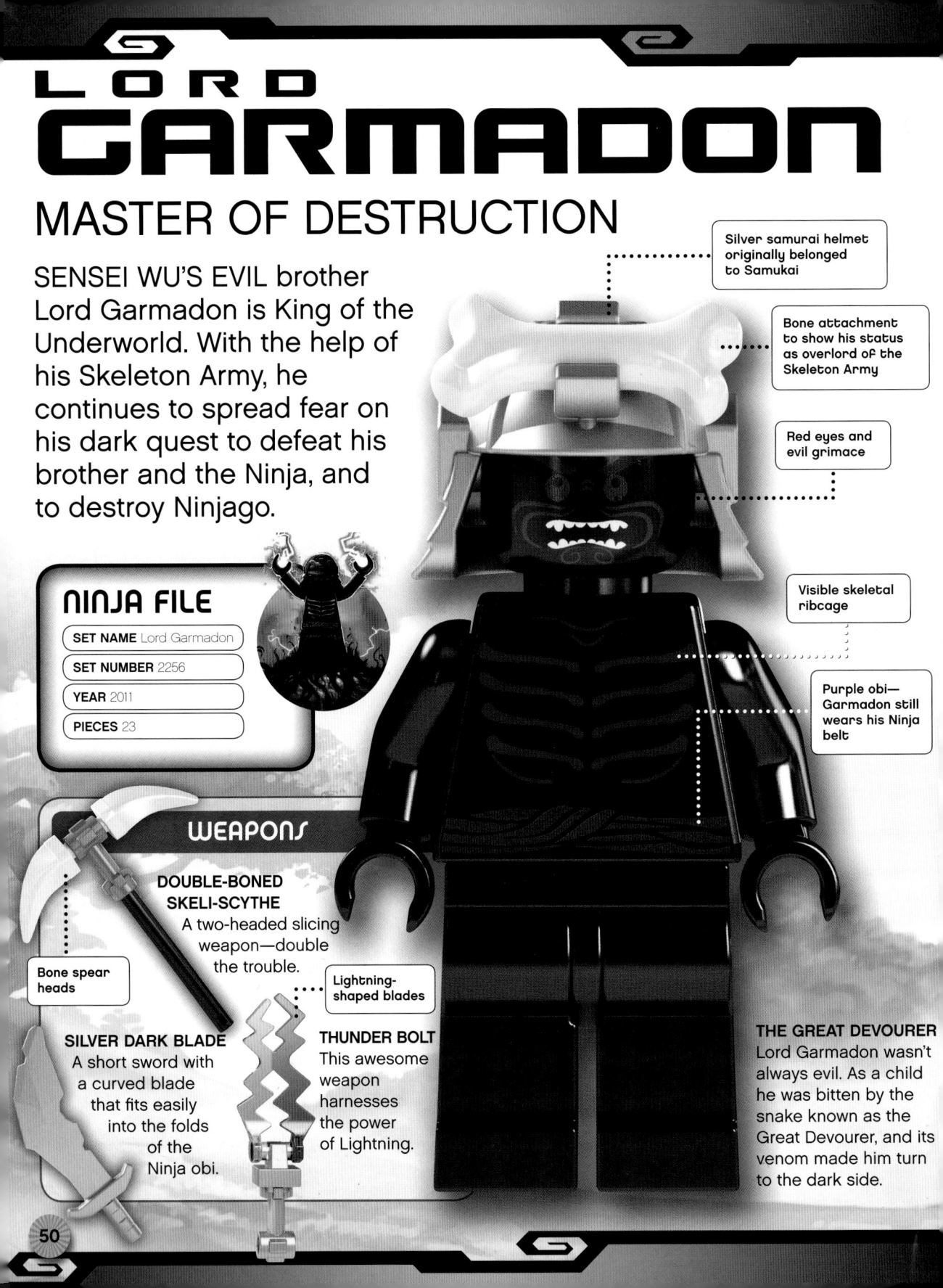

NINJA FILE

SET NAME Lord Garmadon
SET NUMBER 2256
YEAR 2011
PIECES 23

WEAPONS

DOUBLE-BONED SKELI-SCYTHE
A two-headed slicing weapon—double the trouble.

SILVER DARK BLADE
A short sword with a curved blade that fits easily into the folds of the Ninja obi.

THUNDER BOLT
This awesome weapon harnesses the power of Lightning.

THE GREAT DEVOURER
Lord Garmadon wasn't always evil. As a child he was bitten by the snake known as the Great Devourer, and its venom made him turn to the dark side.

SAMUKAI

GENERAL OF FIRE

ONCE THE KING of the Underworld, the fearsome Samukai now leads the Skeleton Army in their battle against the Ninja. Will his hunt for the four Weapons of Spinjitzu be the end of him?

Unique skull markings

Wide, open mouth, unique in LEGO Ninjago minifigures

Four bony arms allow him to wield four weapons at once.

Red skull is the emblem of the Skeleton Army

WEAPONS

SCYTHE OF QUAKES
One of the four mystical Weapons of Spinjitzu.

NUNCHUCKS OF LIGHTNING
Weapon of Spinjitzu powered by a bolt of lightning.

NINJA FILE

SET NAME Garmadon's Dark Fortress/Fire Temple

SET NUMBER 2505/2507

YEAR 2011

PIECES 518/1180

RARE BONES
Samukai is the rarest minifigure in the 2011 LEGO Ninjago range as he only appears in two sets. He is also one of the only three LEGO Ninjago minifigures that don't have spinners.

FRAKJAW

SKELETON OF FIRE

THIS SCARY RED Skeleton is the toughest Skulkin in Lord Garmadon's Army. He is fiery and angry and loves to fight—especially with Ninja!

NINJA FILE

SET NAME SPINJITZU STARTER SET

SET NUMBER 2257

YEAR 2011

PIECES 57

WEAPONS

GOLDEN BATTLE MACE
This golden ball and chain weapon can be deadly.

BONE
Skeletons love to hit their enemies with a long bone!

DARK BLADE
Only the most destructive Skeletons use this brutal weapon.

Body armor includes red shoulder pads

Protective chest plate armor

Skeleton Army emblem

Red combat sash

SKELETON WEAPONS
The Skeletons have a terrifying collection of weapons to use in battle. The Ninja need all their skills to defeat this evil enemy. They are brutal and vicious fighters, and the legendary Frakjaw is one of the worst of all.

EVIL FIRE SPINNER
Frakjaw whirls his golden battle mace to spin up a terrible fiery tornado. He leaves a trail of ash and destruction.

LOUDMOUTH
Frakjaw loves the sound of his own voice and sometimes it is difficult to get him to shut up. He especially likes to taunt and challenge his enemies.

TURBO SHREDDER

BATTLE FOR THE GOLDEN SCYTHE

FRAKJAW DRIVES THIS terrifying Turbo Shredder. This Skeleton tank has a scary skull at the front, fixed between two large caterpillar track treads. The frightening jaws of the skull snap open and closed as the treads move forward, crushing everything in its path... including Ninja!

DID YOU KNOW?
Frakjaw's name is a play on the words "fracture" (a crack or break in a bone) and "jaw"—a suitably sinister combination for this bony evil villain!

NINJA FILE

SET NAME TURBO SHREDDER
SET NUMBER 2263
YEAR 2011
PIECES 223

All-terrain rubber treads

MINIFIGURES
Jay and Cole have to use all their Spinjitzu expertise to avoid being swallowed up by the fang-filled jaws of Frakjaw's Turbo Shredder.

Jay

Cole

Frakjaw

GOLDEN SCYTHE MISSION
Frakjaw has stolen the golden Scythe of Quakes. It is Jay and Cole's mission to get it back before Frakjaw hands it over to the evil Lord Garmadon himself. There's only one problem... Frakjaw is escaping in his fearsome tank. Can the Ninja stop him in time and avoid the tank's terrible fangs?

SNAP ATTACK
Push the Shredder forward on its tire treads. The forward motion pulls upon a lever mechanism that causes the skull's head to move up and down. Watch out for that snapping jaw!

KRAZI

SKELETON OF LIGHTNING

NINJA FILE

SET NAME KRAZI

SET NUMBER 2116

YEAR 2011

PIECES 22

KRAZI BY NAME and crazy by nature, this wild menace is a Skulkin warrior in Lord Garmadon's Skeleton Army. Krazi is the fastest of the Skeletons—when he strikes he is lightning quick. Watch out, he is mad and destructive!

Evil red eyes and crazy red face paint

Blue shoulder pads are part of body armor

Protective chest plate armor

Standard-issue Skeleton Army emblem

WEAPONS

PICKAX
This grim tool is a lethal weapon in the hands (or bones!) of a crazy Skeleton!

DOUBLE-BLADED BONE DAGGER
Twice as dangerous, this double-bladed dark weapon is truly evil. Ninja beware!

GOLDEN BONE
This hard-hitting weapon is simple but effective. Made of gold, it lasts forever!

BONE TERROR
Dangerous and fearless, Krazi is so crazy that he will pick a fight with anyone. He will try to flatten them with his favorite weapon—a large golden bone!

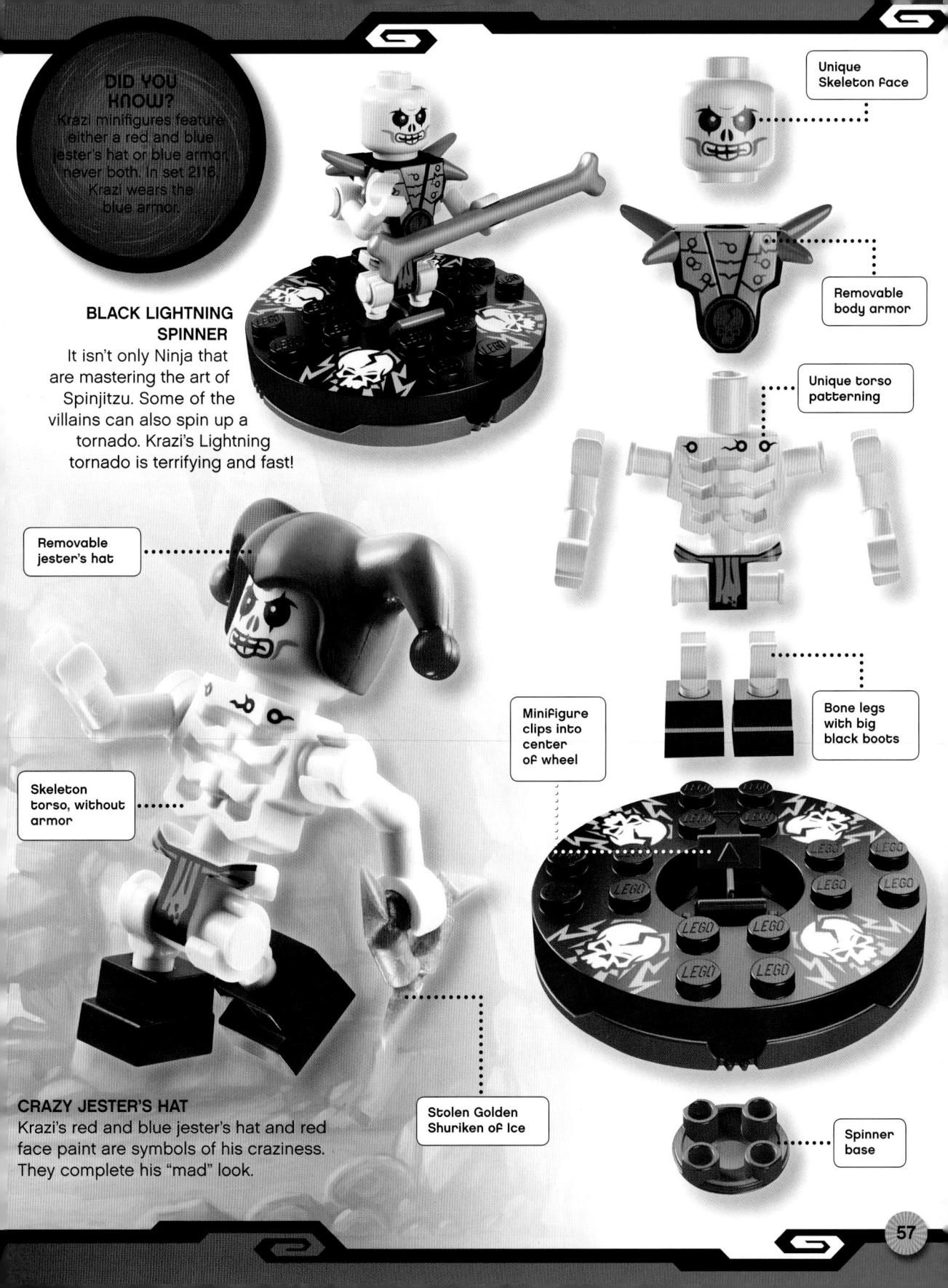

DID YOU KNOW?
Krazi minifigures feature either a red and blue jester's hat or blue armor, never both. In set 2116, Krazi wears the blue armor.

BLACK LIGHTNING SPINNER
It isn't only Ninja that are mastering the art of Spinjitzu. Some of the villains can also spin up a tornado. Krazi's Lightning tornado is terrifying and fast!

CRAZY JESTER'S HAT
Krazi's red and blue jester's hat and red face paint are symbols of his craziness. They complete his "mad" look.

CHOPOV

SKELETON OF EARTH

CHOPOV IS AS tough as a rock. This smart warrior is also the chief mechanic of the Skeleton Army and maintains all of the vehicles. Chopov doesn't let anything get in his way, even Ninja! Beware of his mighty strength.

NINJA FILE

SET NAME CHOPOV
SET NUMBER 2114
YEAR 2011
PIECES 20

Sinister red eyes and battle-scarred face

Protective chest plate armor

Emblem strikes fear into enemies' hearts

Black and gray Ninja-like sash

WEAPONS

GOLDEN DARK BLADE
This golden dark blade is a prized and lethal Skeleton weapon and sister weapon to the dark blade.

BONE
No Skeleton warrior should be without a long striking bone.

STAFF
This battle weapon is effective in the hands of a tough Skulkin!

SKELETON MENACE
Chopov's weapon of choice is the dark blade, but he is skilled with many other weapons, including the bone ax. He secretly wishes that he, instead of Bonezai, could design the Skeleton Army's super cool vehicles.

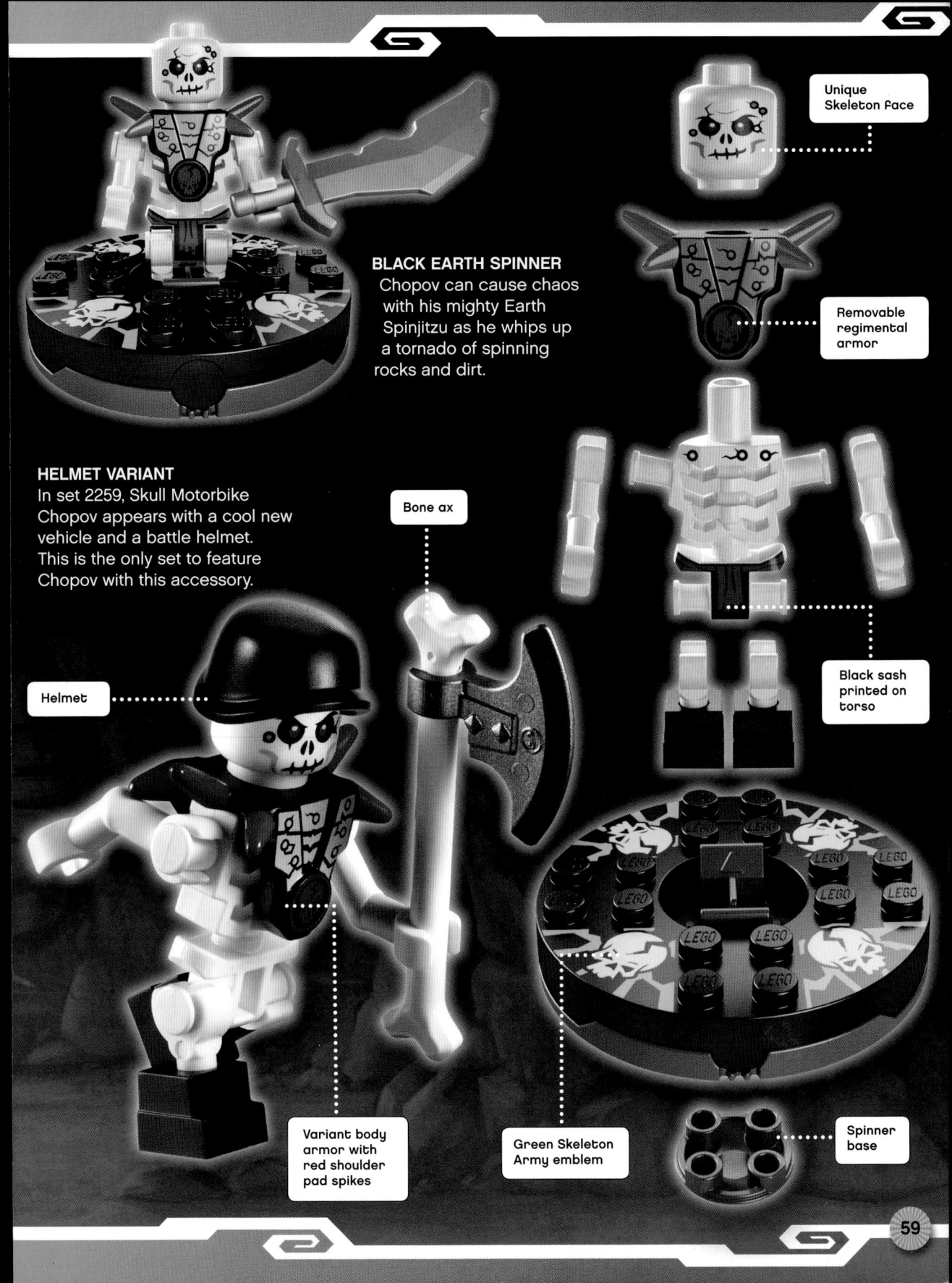

BLACK EARTH SPINNER
Chopov can cause chaos with his mighty Earth Spinjitzu as he whips up a tornado of spinning rocks and dirt.

HELMET VARIANT
In set 2259, Skull Motorbike Chopov appears with a cool new vehicle and a battle helmet. This is the only set to feature Chopov with this accessory.

SKULL MOTORBIKE

NINJA SWAT DEVICE

CHOPOV'S MENACING battle vehicle is a cool chopper motorbike. He uses it in battle or for quick escapes. The powerful skull hammerhead can smash anything in its path, especially Ninja warriors!

NINJA FILE

SET NAME Skull Motorbike

SET NUMBER 2259

YEAR 2011

PIECES 157

Jay

Chopov

MINIFIGURES
Jay battles with Chopov to stop him escaping with the Nunchucks of Lightning. Can he use his Ninja skills to avoid the skull hammerhead?

Catapult hinge mechanism

Double-tired front wheel to keep motorbike stable

BONE CHROME
The Skull Motorbike is equipped with clever bone features: levers, brakes, and horned spikes for knocking over and spearing the enemy. It is an awesome battle vehicle fit for the Skeleton Army.

DID YOU KNOW?
Although Chopov is a loyal member of the Skeleton Army, he secretly hopes that Bonezai will one day be captured in battle so that he can replace him as the vehicle designer.

CATAPULT
Ninja beware! The powerful skull hammerhead catapult on this menacing machine is built to smash almost anything to pieces. Pull down on the lever to activate the catapult arm and knock out the enemy.

BONEZAI

SKELETON OF ICE

BONEZAI DESIGNS ALL the vehicles in the Skeleton Army. This stealthy warrior is as cold as Ice and strikes a chill into the heart of his enemies. Bonezai uses his Ice Element abilities to win weapons and battle for glory.

NINJA FILE

SET NAME BONEZAI

SET NUMBER 2115

YEAR 2011

PIECES 21

Shoulder spikes can be rammed into opponents in battle

Protective body armor protects bony rib cage

Combat sash that Skeleton Army have adopted as part of their uniform

WEAPONS

GOLDEN PICKAX
Made from solid gold, every warrior wants this hard-hitting weapon.

SILVER BONE AX
With its super cutting action, this weapon is lethal in the bony hands of an angry Skeleton!

SILVER BATTLE MACE
Big, heavy, and made of solid silver, this swinging weapon can do some serious damage.

BATTLE CRY!
Bonezai's name is a combination of the Japanese battle cry "banzai" and the word "bone." He is so cold he can even freeze shadows! Watch out for this cool customer, Ninja!

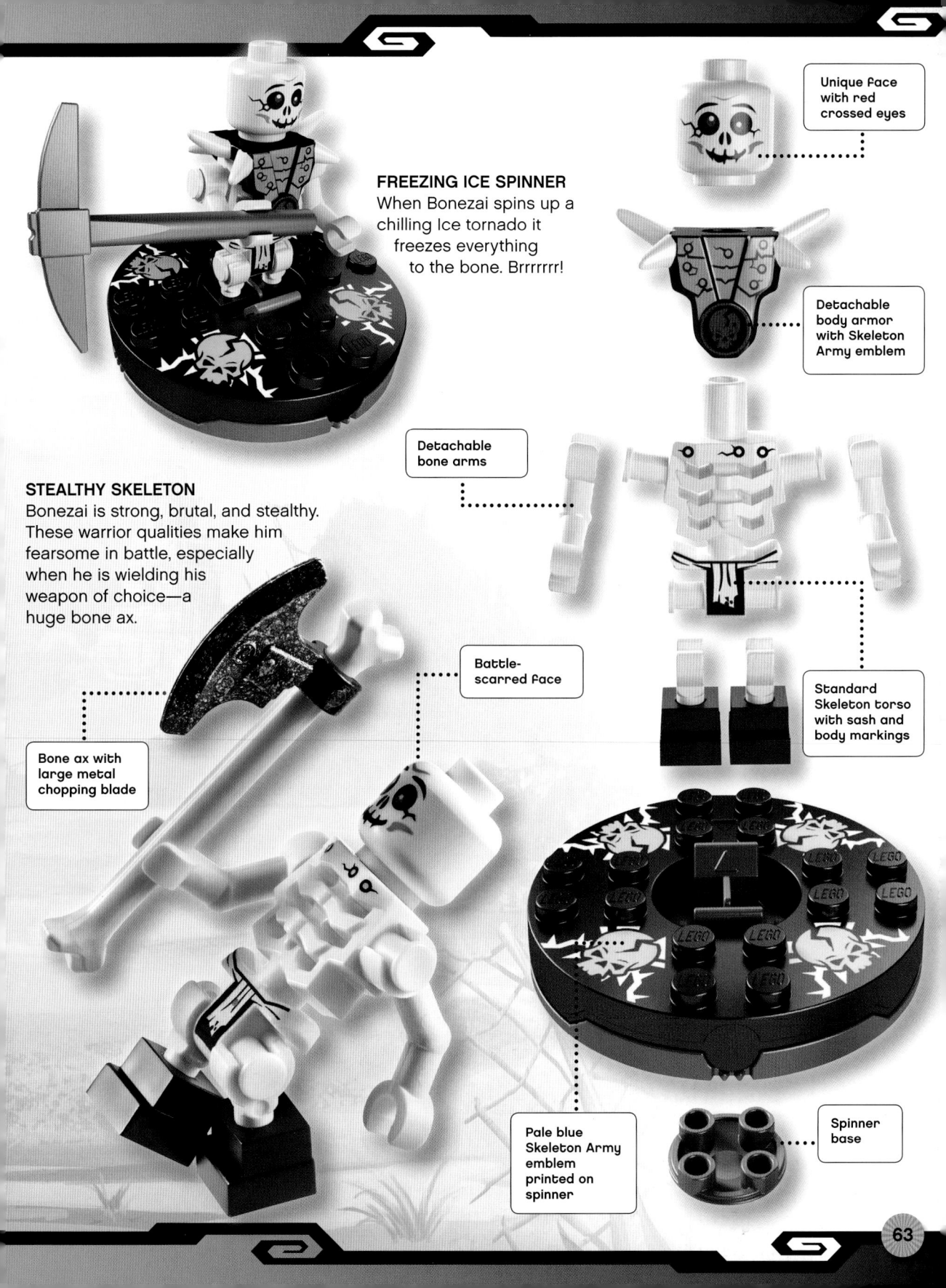

FREEZING ICE SPINNER
When Bonezai spins up a chilling Ice tornado it freezes everything to the bone. Brrrrrrr!

STEALTHY SKELETON
Bonezai is strong, brutal, and stealthy. These warrior qualities make him fearsome in battle, especially when he is wielding his weapon of choice—a huge bone ax.

NINJA BATTLE ARENA

SPIN TO VICTORY!

THIS LIMITED EDITION set is the ultimate test of good versus evil. Earth Ninja Cole must battle the Ice-cold Bonezai for control of the precious Golden Weapons. Spin the minifigures for an epic battle!

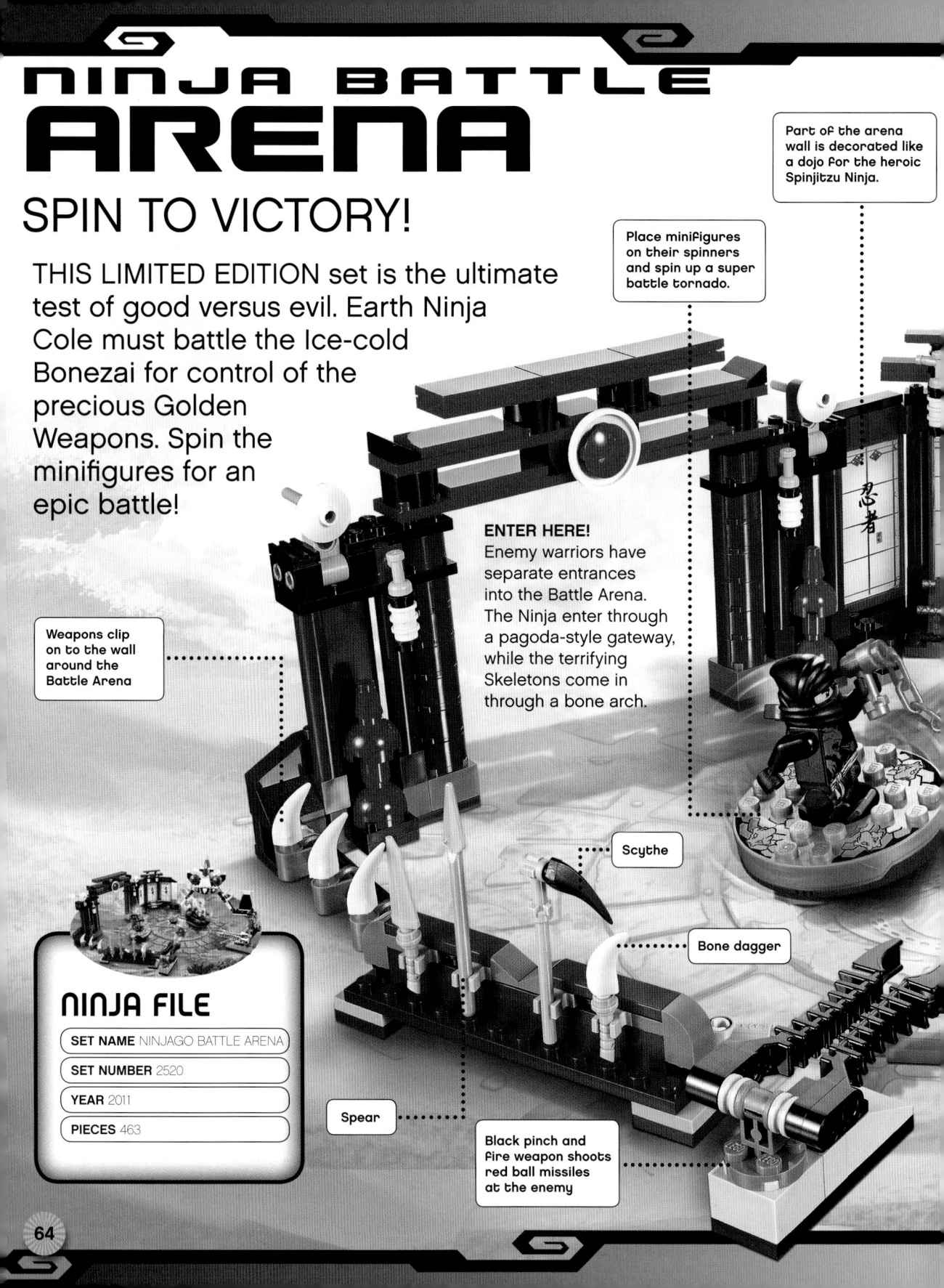

Part of the arena wall is decorated like a dojo for the heroic Spinjitzu Ninja.

Place minifigures on their spinners and spin up a super battle tornado.

ENTER HERE!
Enemy warriors have separate entrances into the Battle Arena. The Ninja enter through a pagoda-style gateway, while the terrifying Skeletons come in through a bone arch.

Weapons clip on to the wall around the Battle Arena

Scythe

Bone dagger

Spear

Black pinch and fire weapon shoots red ball missiles at the enemy

NINJA FILE

SET NAME NINJAGO BATTLE ARENA
SET NUMBER 2520
YEAR 2011
PIECES 463

MINIFIGURES
Who will win this thrilling battle between good and evil? Can Cole overcome Bonezai's cold stealth with his strength and strategic thinking?
Cole DX
Bonezai
ARSENAL OF WEAPONS
This set comes with 14 weapons, including a spiked golden ball. Watch out—the spikes on this missile could be lethal for a brave Ninja or evil Skeleton!
Gray pinch and fire weapon releases spiked golden balls
Ax
Dagger
Ball missile
Golden dark blade
Chainsaw

SKELETON BOWLING

SKELETON STRIKE!

EVEN A NINJA should be no match for six Skeletons. But don't worry, these are just training dummies! Lightning-fast Jay decides to practice his Ninja skills and have some fun at the same time. With nine weapons at his disposal as well as his Spinjitzu spinner, Jay sends the skittles flying.

SPINJITZU FUN!
Jay spins up his tornado and watches as the bones fly all over the training arena! Wall-mounted missiles can also be used to fire red bowling balls at the bony bad guys.

NINJA FILE

SET NAME SKELETON BOWLING
SET NUMBER 2519
YEAR 2011
PIECES 371

MINIFIGURES
Caught in an ambush, Jay uses his Ninja DX skills to turn the situation to his advantage. Six evil Skeletons are no match for this brave Ninja!

Jay DX

PLAY ALONG
How good is your Skeleton bowling? Keep score on this rotating board.
If you hit all six Skeletons, turn the dial to the skull symbol. Nice bowling!

KRUNCHA

GENERAL OF EARTH

LOUD, HARD, AND strong, Kruncha is one of the four Generals in the Skeleton Army. He is constantly bickering with General Nuckal. Kruncha is mean and will crush anyone who dares to get in his way.

NINJA FILE

SET NAME KRUNCHA

SET NUMBER 2174

YEAR 2011

PIECES 24

Kruncha wears a monocle on his right eye.

Chest plate with added protection for Skeleton Generals

WEAPONS

CHAINED FANG
A dinosaur tooth on a steel chain is perfect for piercing an enemy in battle.

GOLDEN HATCHET TWINS
This double-bladed golden weapon is twice as deadly as a regular ax.

BONE
Every Skeleton likes to have a big bone weapon to wield in battle.

BODY ARMOR
Kruncha's protective body armor is different from that of most other Skeletons. The shoulder pads are heavier and he doesn't wear the gray chest panel with markings on it. Only Wyplash has similar armor to Kruncha's.

ROCK HARD SPINJITZU
Kruncha is cold, mean, smart, and hard as rock. Even his own soldiers in the Skeleton Army are scared of him. He is a force to be reckoned with when he spins up his tornado of crushing rocks and dirt.

ARMY POSITION
Kruncha is second-in-command to Samukai in the Skeleton Army. He uses the power of his position to make sure the other Skeletons know who is in charge.

DID YOU KNOW?
Kruncha, like Nuckal, was a teacher for a short while, at Darkley's Boarding School for Bad Boys. Lloyd Garmadon is a pupil there, but he runs away.

SKULLCOPTER

RESCUE MISSION

THE SKULKINS ARE armed and dangerous! When Jay and the Lightning Dragon try to attack the Skullcopter to rescue their master Sensei Wu, Frackjaw and Kruncha flick-fire skull head missiles at them. Ouch! Those bone heads are hard and lethal.

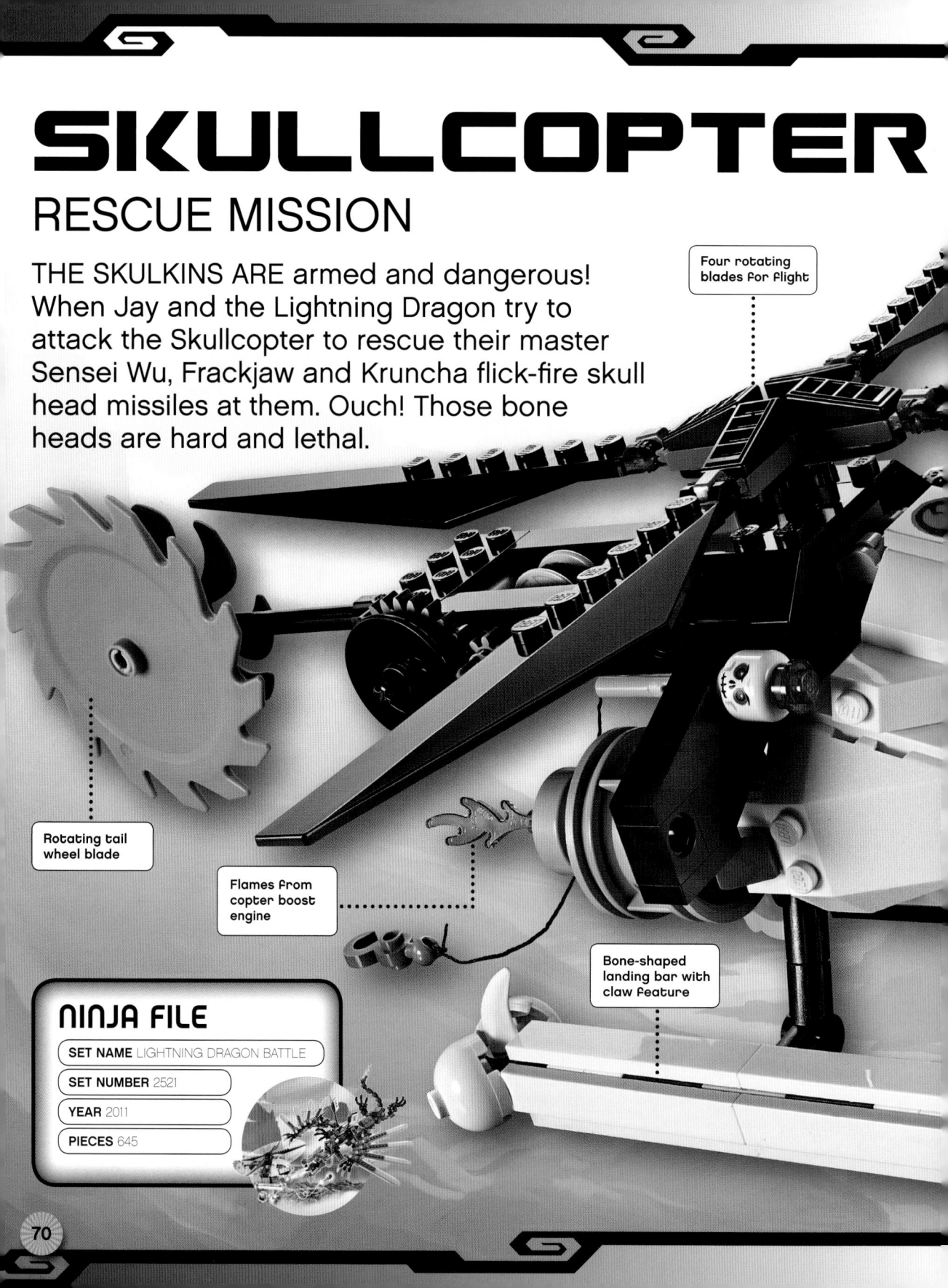

NINJA FILE

SET NAME LIGHTNING DRAGON BATTLE

SET NUMBER 2521

YEAR 2011

PIECES 645

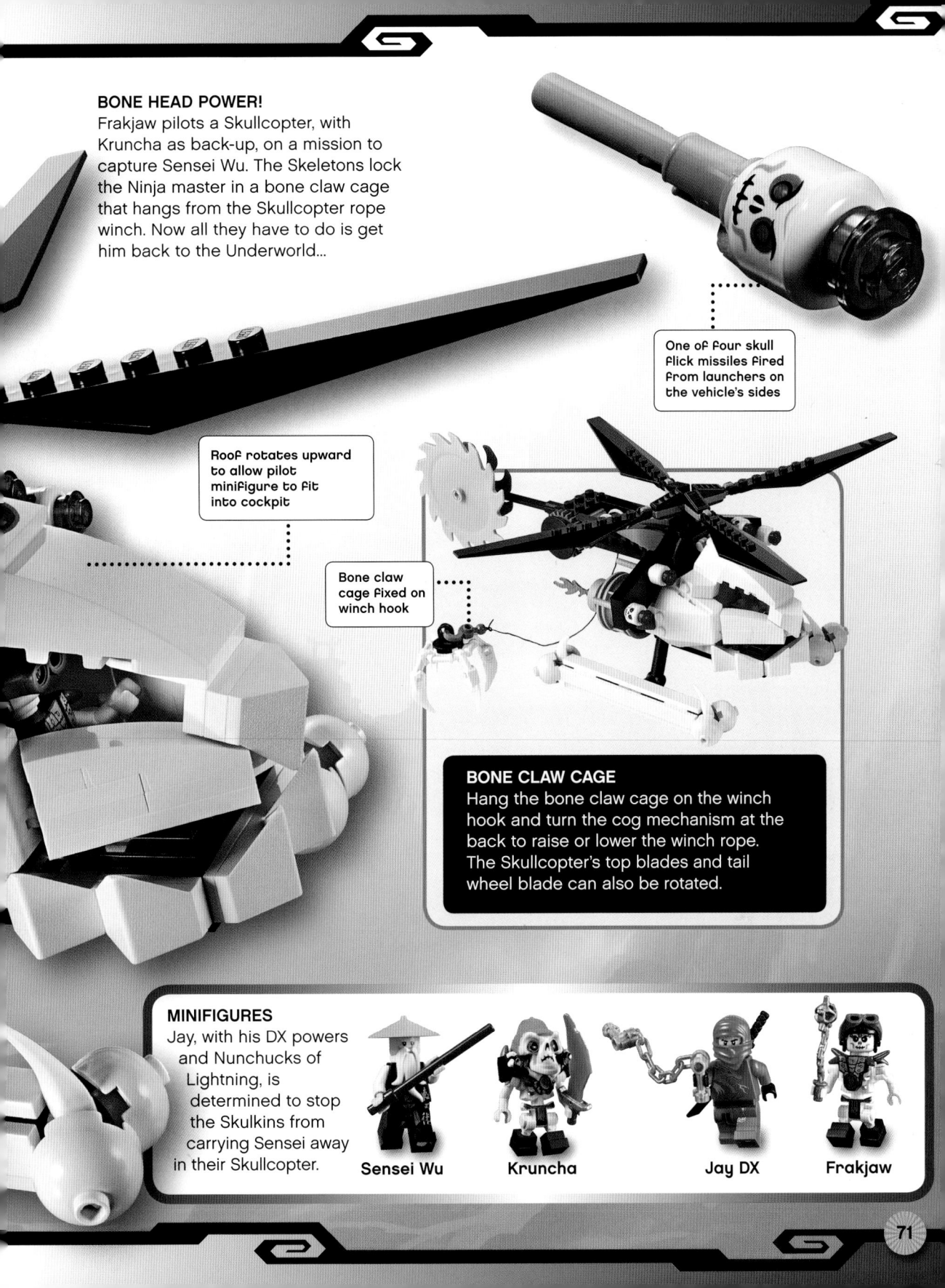

BONE HEAD POWER!
Frakjaw pilots a Skullcopter, with Kruncha as back-up, on a mission to capture Sensei Wu. The Skeletons lock the Ninja master in a bone claw cage that hangs from the Skullcopter rope winch. Now all they have to do is get him back to the Underworld...

One of four skull flick missiles fired from launchers on the vehicle's sides

Roof rotates upward to allow pilot minifigure to fit into cockpit

Bone claw cage fixed on winch hook

BONE CLAW CAGE
Hang the bone claw cage on the winch hook and turn the cog mechanism at the back to raise or lower the winch rope. The Skullcopter's top blades and tail wheel blade can also be rotated.

MINIFIGURES
Jay, with his DX powers and Nunchucks of Lightning, is determined to stop the Skulkins from carrying Sensei away in their Skullcopter.

Sensei Wu

Kruncha

Jay DX

Frakjaw

WYPLASH

GENERAL OF ICE

THIS FEARSOME SKELETON is a General in Garmadon's Army. He even takes control of the Army in Samukai's absence. Stealth is his special skill, and he always watches and waits for the right moment to attack his enemy.

DID YOU KNOW?
Wyplash can turn his huge skull backward! This is a useful skill when you are as paranoid as he is—he can always see the enemy approaching.

NINJA FILE

SET NAME WYPLASH
SET NUMBER 2175
YEAR 2011
PIECES 23

UNDERWORLD SPY
Wyplash is so stealthy that he can creep up on his enemies unseen. This makes him an ideal spy. He watches and listens, gathering information to plan an attack or set up an ambush.

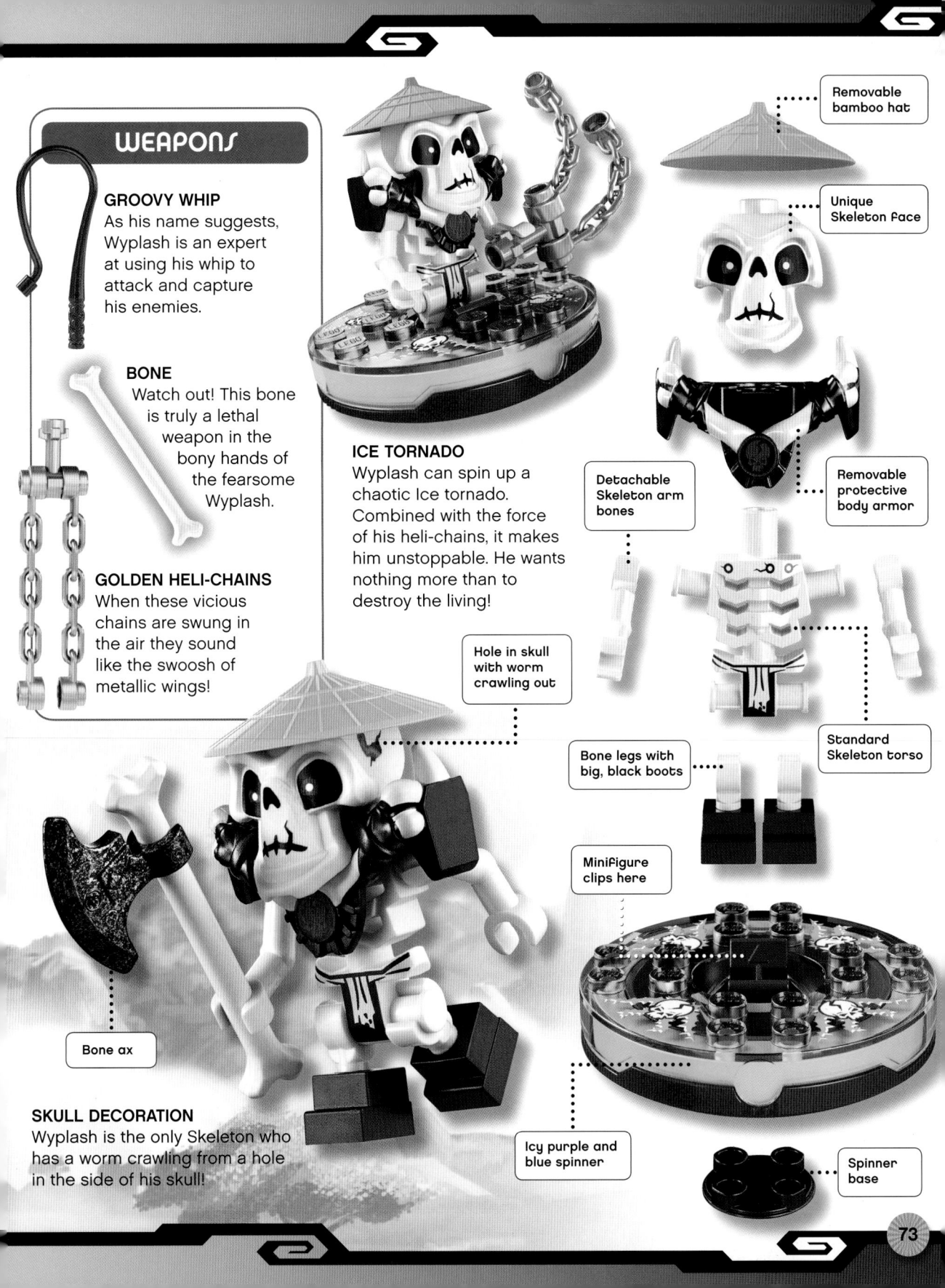
WEAPONS
GROOVY WHIP
As his name suggests, Wyplash is an expert at using his whip to attack and capture his enemies.
BONE
Watch out! This bone is truly a lethal weapon in the bony hands of the fearsome Wyplash.
GOLDEN HELI-CHAINS
When these vicious chains are swung in the air they sound like the swoosh of metallic wings!
ICE TORNADO
Wyplash can spin up a chaotic Ice tornado. Combined with the force of his heli-chains, it makes him unstoppable. He wants nothing more than to destroy the living!
Removable bamboo hat
Unique Skeleton face
Detachable Skeleton arm bones
Removable protective body armor
Hole in skull with worm crawling out
Standard Skeleton torso
Bone legs with big, black boots
Minifigure clips here
Bone ax
SKULL DECORATION
Wyplash is the only Skeleton who has a worm crawling from a hole in the side of his skull!
Icy purple and blue spinner
Spinner base

SKULL TRUCK

MONSTER VEHICLE

THE MONSTROUS Skull Truck is intended to scare even the bravest Ninja. Its hood takes the form of a skull, with jaws that can chomp down on anything or anyone that gets in the way. And if the jaws don't catch them, then the bone fist missile might!

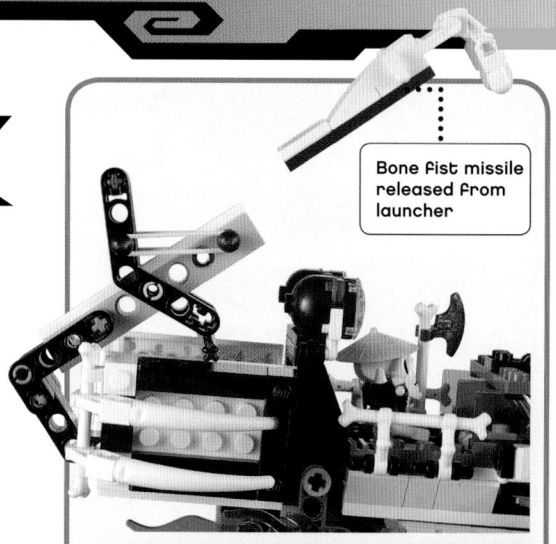

BONE LAUNCHER
Position, aim, and pull down on the moving hinged launcher device at the back of the Skull Truck to let loose the hard-hitting bone fist missile!

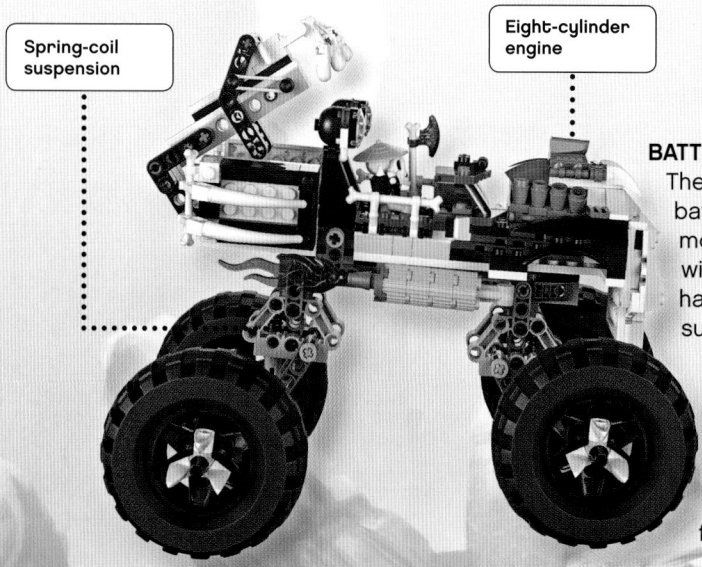

Large, all-terrain rubber tires

BATTLE BEAST!
The Skull Truck is an ideal battle vehicle as it can move over any terrain with ease. Its huge wheels have a built-in spring-coil suspension. The springing movement pushes the truck body up and down on its rubber tires and, at the same time, operates the crushing jaws of the skull at the front of the vehicle.

MINIFIGURES
Lord Garmadon and Wyplash are escaping in the Skull Truck with the Nunchucks of Lightning. Can Jay and Zane stop them?

Wyplash

Jay

Zane

Lord Garmadon

NINJA FILE

SET NAME SKULL TRUCK

SET NUMBER 2506

YEAR 2011

PIECES 515

PRISONER TRANSPORTATION
The bone teeth cages at the back of the Truck are ideal for transporting enemy prisoners. Lift the bone bars and place a minifigure into the base, and then push the teeth back down to lock in the captive.

NUCKAL

GENERAL OF LIGHTNING

NUCKAL IS CHILDISH, wild, and very dangerous. He loves fighting, and if there is trouble to be found, Nuckal will find it! Watch out Ninja—this bony brute can strike you down with his lightning-fast moves and his bony battle skills.

DID YOU KNOW?
The four Skeleton Generals, Nuckal, Samukai, Wyplash, and Kruncha are the only Skeleton minifigures to have proper skull-shaped head pieces.

Unique row of head spikes

Blue shoulder spikes, part of protective body armor

Huge, distinctive skull-shaped head

Skeleton Army emblem

Bone legs with black boots clipped to torso.

NINJA FILE

SET NAME NUCKAL

SET NUMBER 2173

YEAR 2011

PIECES 26

SMASHING FUN!
Nuckal loves having fun, but his idea of fun is fighting and smashing things up! His cackling and electrifying laugh is terrifying, especially when he is wielding a lethal weapon at the same time.

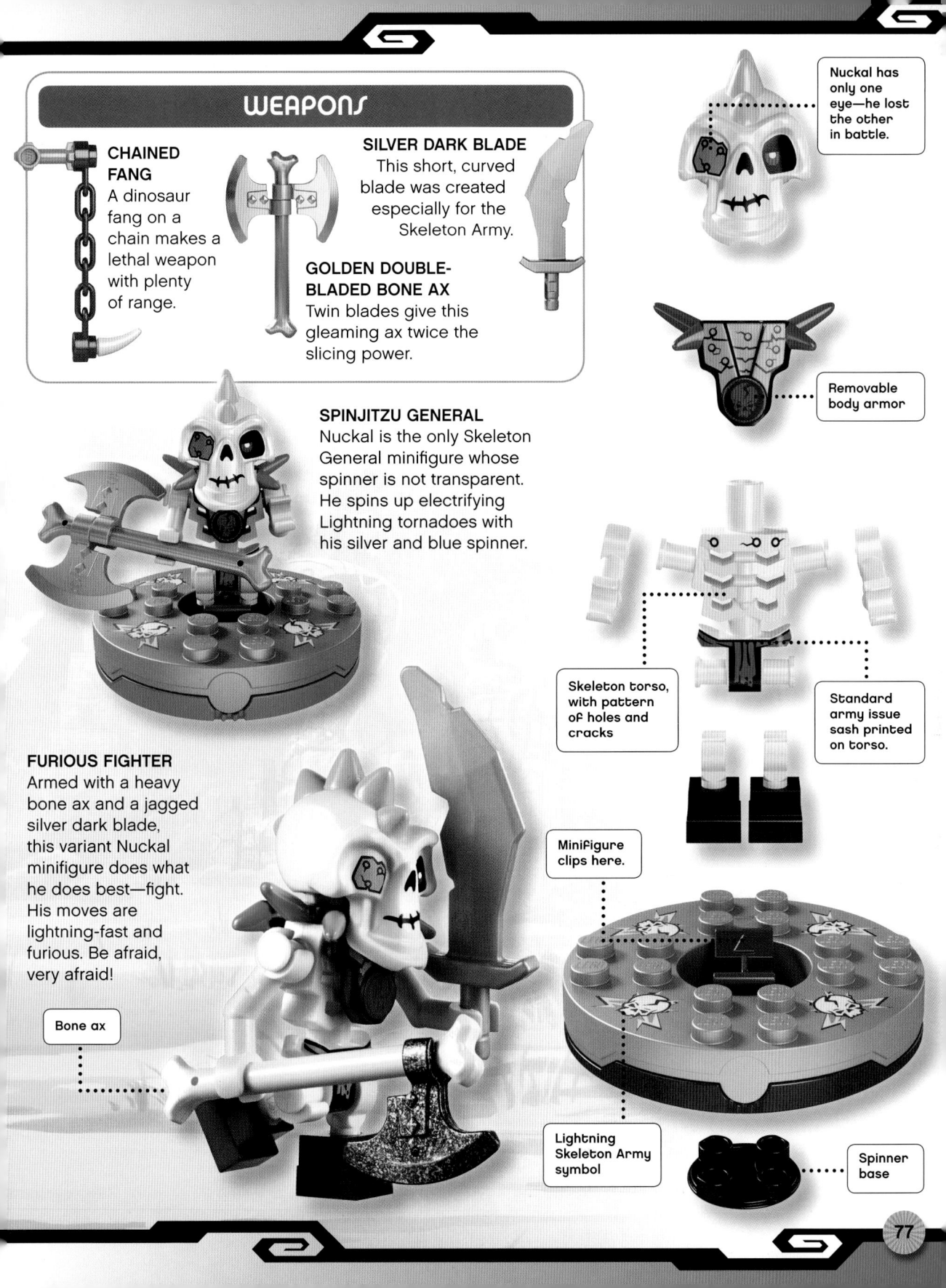
WEAPONS
CHAINED FANG
A dinosaur fang on a chain makes a lethal weapon with plenty of range.
SILVER DARK BLADE
This short, curved blade was created especially for the Skeleton Army.
GOLDEN DOUBLE-BLADED BONE AX
Twin blades give this gleaming ax twice the slicing power.
Nuckal has only one eye—he lost the other in battle.
Removable body armor
SPINJITZU GENERAL
Nuckal is the only Skeleton General minifigure whose spinner is not transparent. He spins up electrifying Lightning tornadoes with his silver and blue spinner.
Skeleton torso, with pattern of holes and cracks
Standard army issue sash printed on torso.
FURIOUS FIGHTER
Armed with a heavy bone ax and a jagged silver dark blade, this variant Nuckal minifigure does what he does best—fight. His moves are lightning-fast and furious. Be afraid, very afraid!
Minifigure clips here.
Bone ax
Lightning Skeleton Army symbol
Spinner base

NUCKAL'S ATV

MISSION IMPOSSIBLE?

NINJA, WATCH OUT! Nuckal's monster All-Terrain Vehicle (ATV) causes maximum destruction wherever it goes. This scary bone buggy packs a punch with its heavy armor, solid suspension, and missile launcher. It is to be avoided at all costs!

NINJA FILE

SET NAME NUCKAL'S ATV

SET NUMBER 2518

YEAR 2011

PIECES 174

MINIFIGURES
Nuckal is trying to capture Nya. Can Kai use his Spinjitzu skills to stop Nuckal and save his sister?

Nuckal

Kai DX

Empty missile launcher

Skull hood piece moves up and down

Fiery exhaust flame

Missile loaded in launcher

ALL-TERRAIN VEHICLE
Nuckal certainly has the advantage on the battlefield with this terrifying four-wheeled vehicle. The ATV has full body armor for protection, and a missile launcher for causing serious damage. The spiked wheels and suspension mean Nuckal can tear up and over any terrain.

BUILT TO BATTLE
Nuckal's favorite pastime is fighting and smashing things up, so this is the perfect vehicle for him. With his lightning-fast agility, he can maneuver this bony beast of a machine with skill and precision!

ALL-TERRAIN MISSILES
Aim and hit the red button behind the skull head to launch this lethal rocket torpedo. Kai will have to use all his Ninja skills to avoid this explosive device.

DARK FORTRESS

GARMADON'S LAIR

THE SCENE IS set for an epic battle between good and evil. The Ninja must rescue three of the Golden Weapons, but will they get past the terrifying defenses of Lord Garmadon's Underworld Fortress?

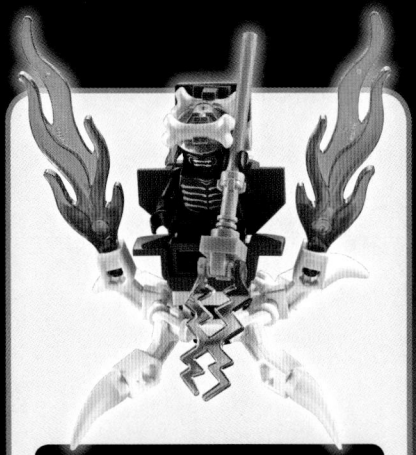

MOVING THRONE
Only the Lord of Evil could have a flying bone throne! Garmadon will be hot on the Ninja's trail with this flame powered vehicle, if they manage to escape...

GRAVE SURPRISE!
The Fortress is full of horrible surprises! Be prepared for a bony scare if you press on the red hinge—up pops a skeleton. Argh!

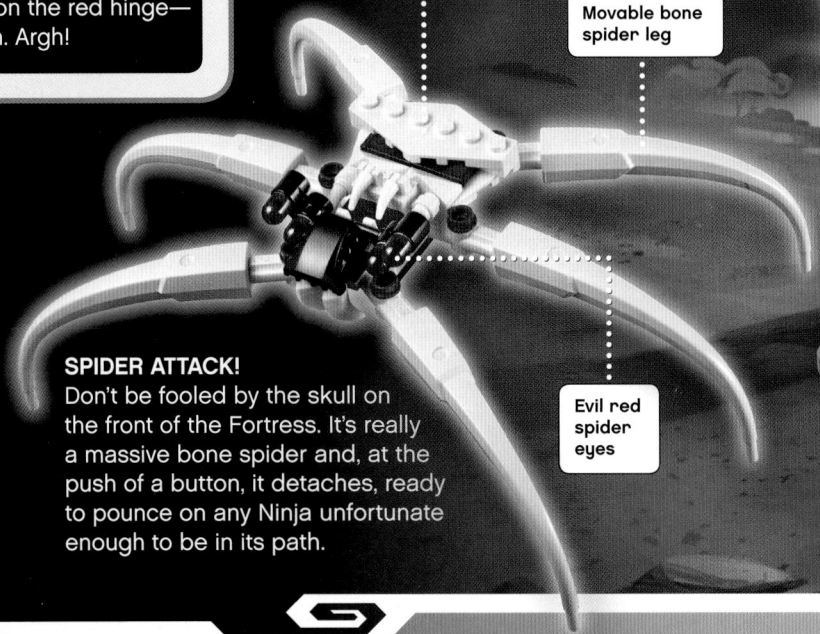

SPIDER ATTACK!
Don't be fooled by the skull on the front of the Fortress. It's really a massive bone spider and, at the push of a button, it detaches, ready to pounce on any Ninja unfortunate enough to be in its path.

NINJA FILE

SET NAME Garmadon's Dark Fortress

SET NUMBER 2505

YEAR 2011

PIECES 518

MINIFIGURES
Kai and Nya will have to use all their skills to get past the Fortress's massive spider and flick missiles before they battle the Skeletons.

EVIL LAIR
Buried deep in the Underworld, Lord Garmadon's Fortress is filled with evil secrets and sinister shadows.

WEAPONS

BOTH THE NINJA warriors and the Skeleton Army have an incredible collection of weapons. It takes special skills to wield them and lots of practice to master them. Before going into battle a Ninja or Skeleton must evaluate his enemy and decide which weapon, or weapons, will help him win.

MACES

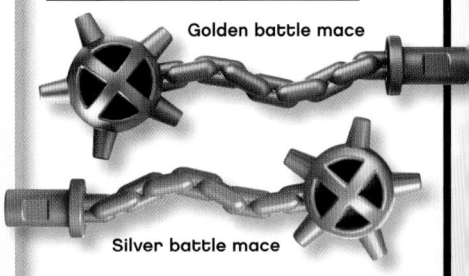

Swing these spikes at your foe, but be careful not to hit yourself!

SWORDS

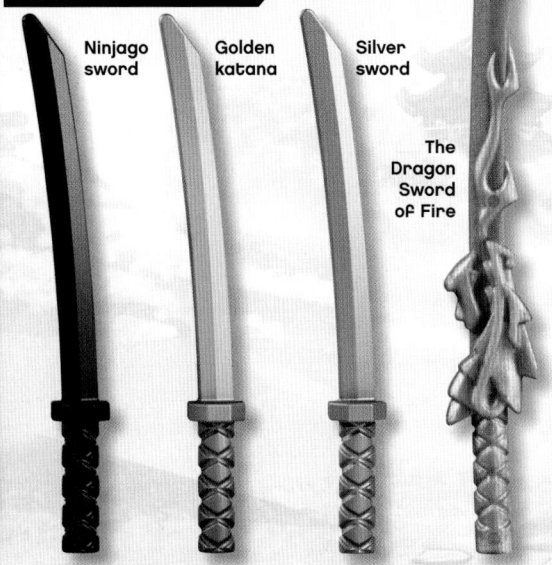

The katana sword is a traditional Ninja weapon and must only be used by experts.

DARK BLADES

These jagged blades are more stylish than a regular dagger but also much heavier!

THUNDER BOLT

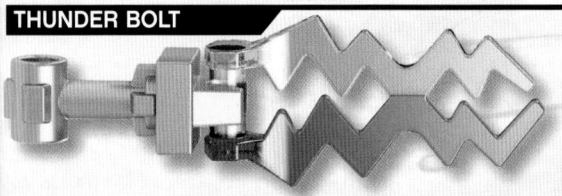

Made from two bolts of lightning, this sizzling weapon can sometimes be too hot to handle.

SCYTHE BLADE

This curved blade is more commonly seen on a longer scythe weapon.

AXES

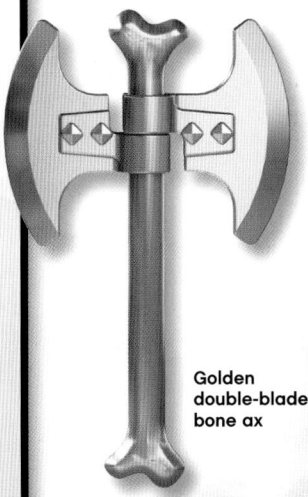

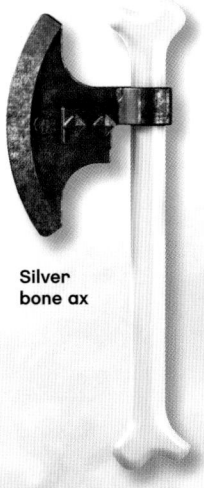

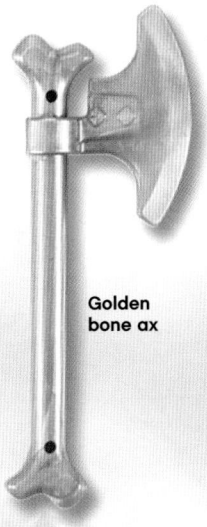

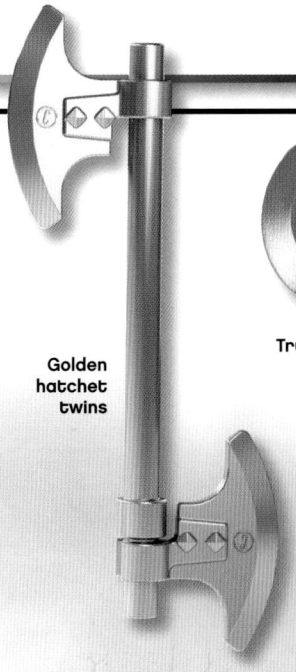

Chop chop! These trusty old weapons can also be used to chop firewood.

DARK TALONS

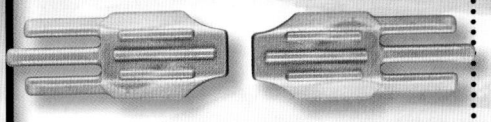

These weapons fit over a minifigure's hands for close combat situations.

PICKAXES

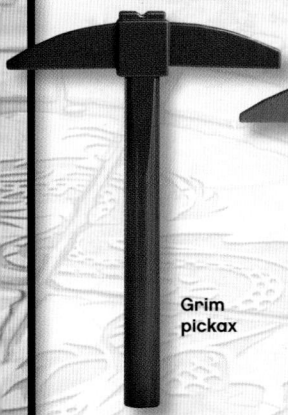

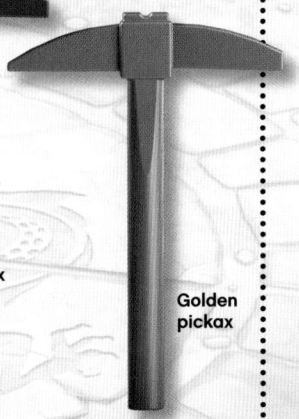

Axes make an excellent weapon or a useful tool.

SPEARS

Long and very heavy, these spears can only be wielded by the strongest Ninja or Skulkins.

SCYTHES

Scythe of Quakes

Double-boned skeli-scythe

Double-bladed scythe

Bone scythe

Scythes can be used for cutting down crops on the field, or opponents on the battlefield.

DAGGERS

Golden nick dagger

Silver nick dagger

Dragon's breath dagger

Bone dagger

Double-bladed bone dagger

Double-bladed dagger

Gold-tipped, breathing fire, or double-bladed, there is a dagger to suit every kind of battle!

BLACKSMITH'S HAMMER

Blunt and heavy, a hammer is great for banging in nails, or whacking enemies on the head.

SHURIKENS OF ICE

Beware of these beautiful throwing stars, they are extremely sharp!

BONES

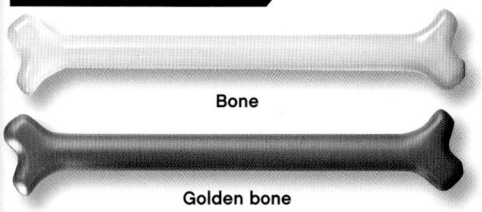

A Skeleton favorite, bones are brilliant for bashing and banging.

CHAIN SAW

Stay away from this sharp, buzzing weapon, unless you have a tree to cut down.

GROOVY WHIP

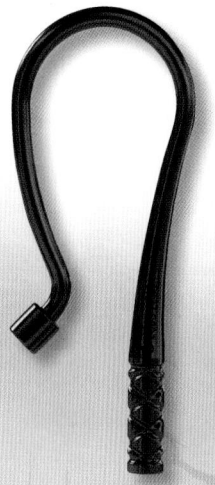

This is made from a vicious vine that grasps its victims and never lets go!

STAFFS

Staffs are simple weapons and if you are not in a battle, they make a handy walking stick.

CHAIN WEAPONS

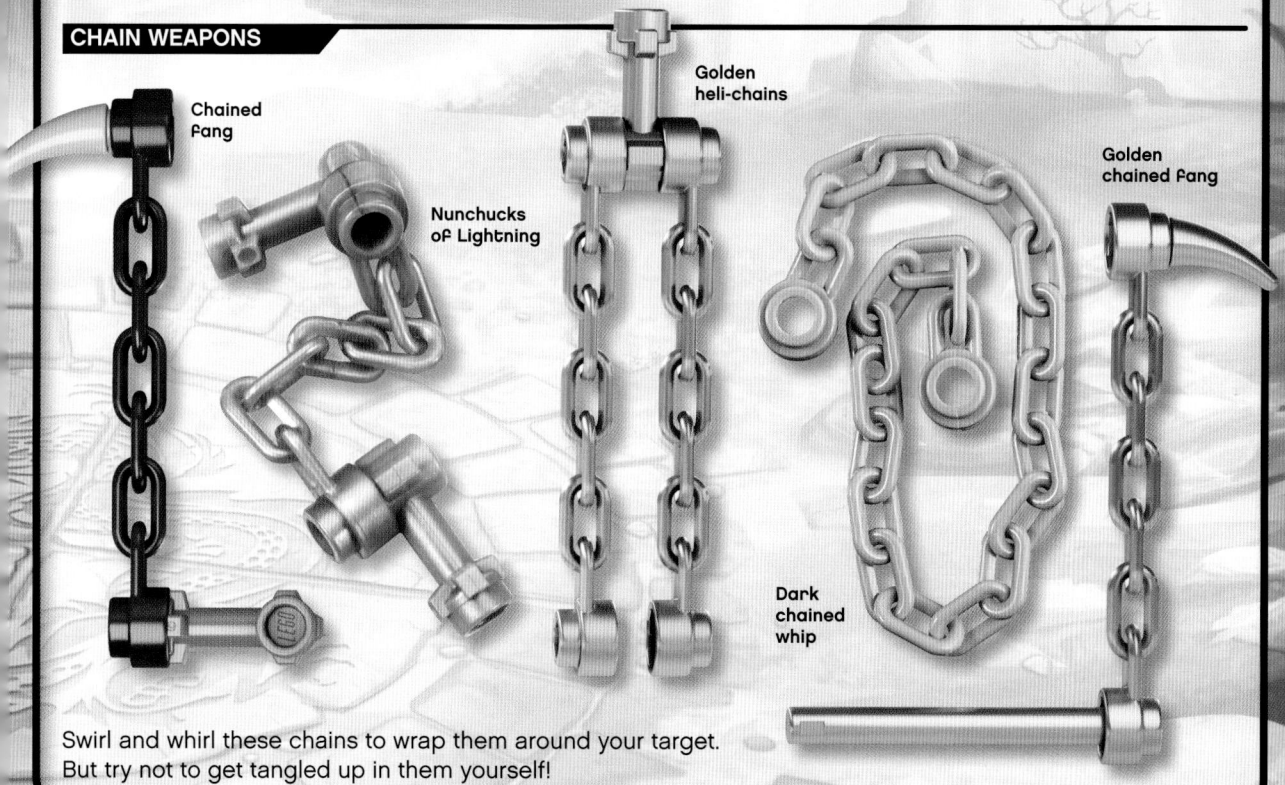

Swirl and whirl these chains to wrap them around your target. But try not to get tangled up in them yourself!

FINAL BATTLE

AT THE DARK FORTRESS

THE SKELETONS HAVE stolen three of the Golden Weapons. Sensei Wu and the Ninja bravely go to Lord Garmadon's Underworld lair to get them back. They must stop the dark Lord uniting all four Weapons and destroying Ninjago.

ATTACK! The Ninja confront the Skeleton Army at Lord Garmadon's Dark Fortress. The Skeletons have an arsenal of evil weapons and missiles. Watch out for the skull thrower missiles, Ninja!

FIGHT! During an epic battle between the Skeletons and the Ninja, the clever Ninja combine their elemental powers to make a mighty Tornado of Creation. With Nya's help, they destroy the Skeleton Army and make their way to Garmadon's Fortress throne room. Bye bye you bags of bones!

DUEL! Sensei Wu and Samukai fight for possession of the four Golden Weapons. Samukai wins. However, the combined power of the Weapons is too great, and Samukai is destroyed. So long, Samukai!

Garmadon escapes into the vortex on his flying throne.
The Dark Fortress
Kai spins a fiery tornado.
Samukai battles for possession of the four Golden Weapons.
UH OH! The awesome power of the Golden Weapons opens up a mysterious vortex to another world. Lord Garmadon escapes into this vortex. But don't worry, he'll be back to get revenge on his brother one day...

NINJA VS. SERPENTINE
SEASON TWO OF LEGO® Ninjago sees the return of Lord Garmadon from the Underworld. Plus, a new enemy is unleashed—the Serpentine. A total of fourteen amazing LEGO sets bring the action to life. Turn the page and learn about all the characters, weapons, vehicles, and locations—and meet a very special Ninja...

DON'T SSSPEAK TOO SSSOON, NINJA!
WE WILL STOP YOU AND YOUR KIND!

A NEW ADVENTURE

Peace in the land of Ninjago did not last very long. Lord Garmadon has returned from the Underworld. This time he is stronger than before and has the power to control all four Golden Weapons. But the Ninja are stronger too, and Cole, Jay, Kai, and Zane will do everything they can to protect these powerful Weapons...

While Lord Garmadon lurks in the shadows, waiting for the right moment to strike, the Ninja meet his young son, Lloyd Garmadon. The mischievous Lloyd carelessly unleashes a fearsome new enemy upon Ninjago—the mysterious and ancient Serpentine tribes.

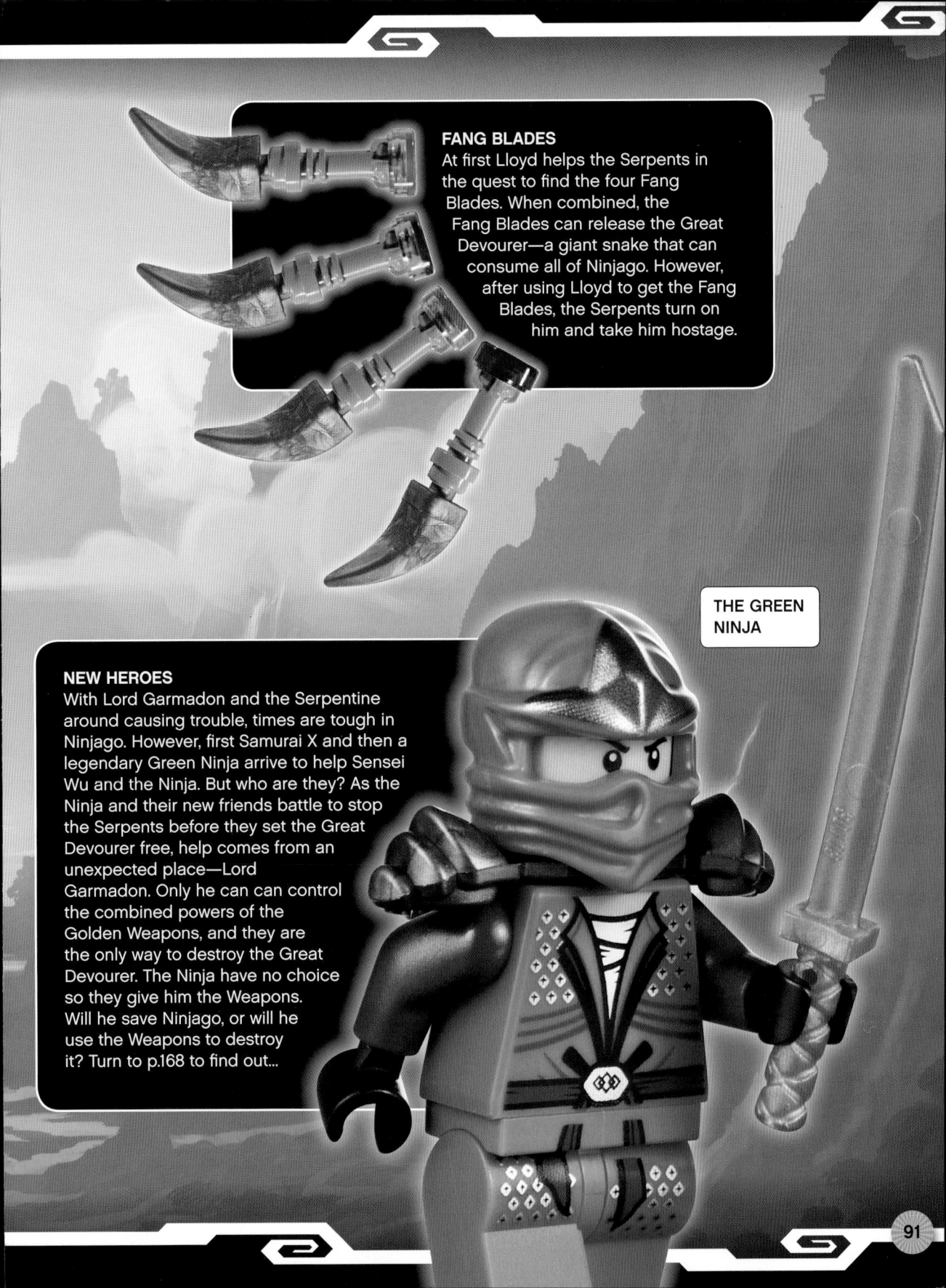

FANG BLADES
At first Lloyd helps the Serpents in the quest to find the four Fang Blades. When combined, the Fang Blades can release the Great Devourer—a giant snake that can consume all of Ninjago. However, after using Lloyd to get the Fang Blades, the Serpents turn on him and take him hostage.

THE GREEN NINJA

NEW HEROES
With Lord Garmadon and the Serpentine around causing trouble, times are tough in Ninjago. However, first Samurai X and then a legendary Green Ninja arrive to help Sensei Wu and the Ninja. But who are they? As the Ninja and their new friends battle to stop the Serpents before they set the Great Devourer free, help comes from an unexpected place—Lord Garmadon. Only he can can control the combined powers of the Golden Weapons, and they are the only way to destroy the Great Devourer. The Ninja have no choice so they give him the Weapons. Will he save Ninjago, or will he use the Weapons to destroy it? Turn to p.168 to find out...

SENSEI WU

NINJA TEACHER

THE CALM AND self-disciplined Sensei Wu is the perfect teacher. After years of training, he knows what it takes to master Spinjitzu and the Elements. He uses this knowledge to teach the Ninja and help them to reach the next three levels—ZX (Zen eXtreme), Kendo, and NRG.

NINJA FILE

SET NAME DESTINY'S BOUNTY

SET NUMBER 9446

YEAR 2012

PIECES 684

MASTER OF THE ELEMENTS

Sensei Wu knows how to bring out the best in the young Ninja. He trains each of them in one of the four Elements of Ninjago—Earth, Lightning, Fire, or Ice. The four Elements are powerful forces that can be harnessed for good or evil. The Ninja can control these Elements, but so can the evil Lord Garmadon and his Skeleton Army.

Traditional conical bamboo sun hat

"Sensei" mustache and beard

Sensei Wu's alternative white robes feature snake symbols to protect him from evil.

Gray obi sash belt

THE FOUR ELEMENTS

Each Ninja is assigned one of the Elements and must train hard to master it. Sensei Wu identifies the Ninja's individual skills and helps them harness the Elements in their own way.

FIRE

Kai's elemental power is Fire. His personality is wild and intense like a fire. He can be reckless and impatient and quick to anger.

EARTH

Cole's elemental power is Earth. He may be a bit gruff, but he is strong, focused, reliable, and solid as a rock.

DID YOU KNOW?

Lord Garmadon has the ability to command all four of the Elements, just like his little brother, Sensei Wu. Unlike Wu, however, Garmadon's grasp of the elemental forces is unbalanced, a sign of his inner evil.

LIGHTNING

Jay's elemental power is Lightning. He is creative, brave, has a great sense of humor, and is lightning-fast in combat.

ICE

Zane's elemental power is Ice. He is serious, stealthy, and focused. He is always cool under pressure.

DESTINY'S BOUNTY

NINJA HEADQUARTERS

DESTINY'S BOUNTY IS the Ninja's new home and training center. The dragon-themed ship comes fully equipped with a cannon with a 360 degree firing range, four crossbows, two concealed weapon compartments, and a hidden treasure chest with jewels inside. All aboard!

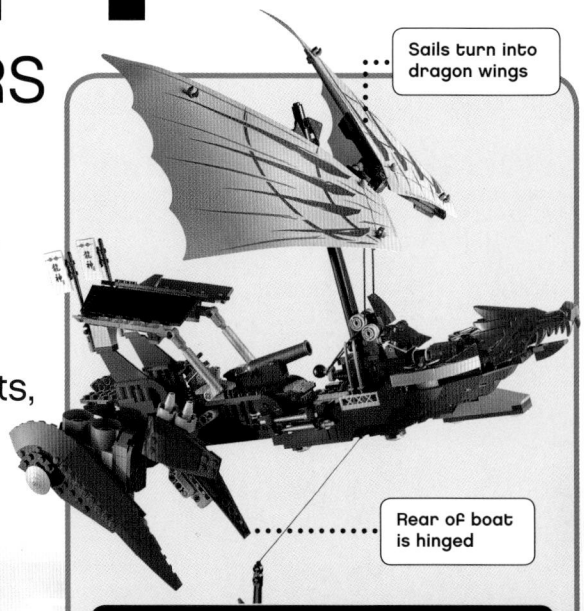

DESTINY JET
Destiny's Bounty hides a few surprises—the stern (rear end) twists down to convert the ship into a flying machine. The red blade-like side panels become the booster engines to power the Destiny Jet.

NINJA FILE

SET NAME DESTINY'S BOUNTY
SET NUMBER 9446
YEAR 2012
PIECES 684

LEVERAGE
A clever system of ropes and pulleys, operated by a turning lever, opens and closes the sails for flight or sail mode.

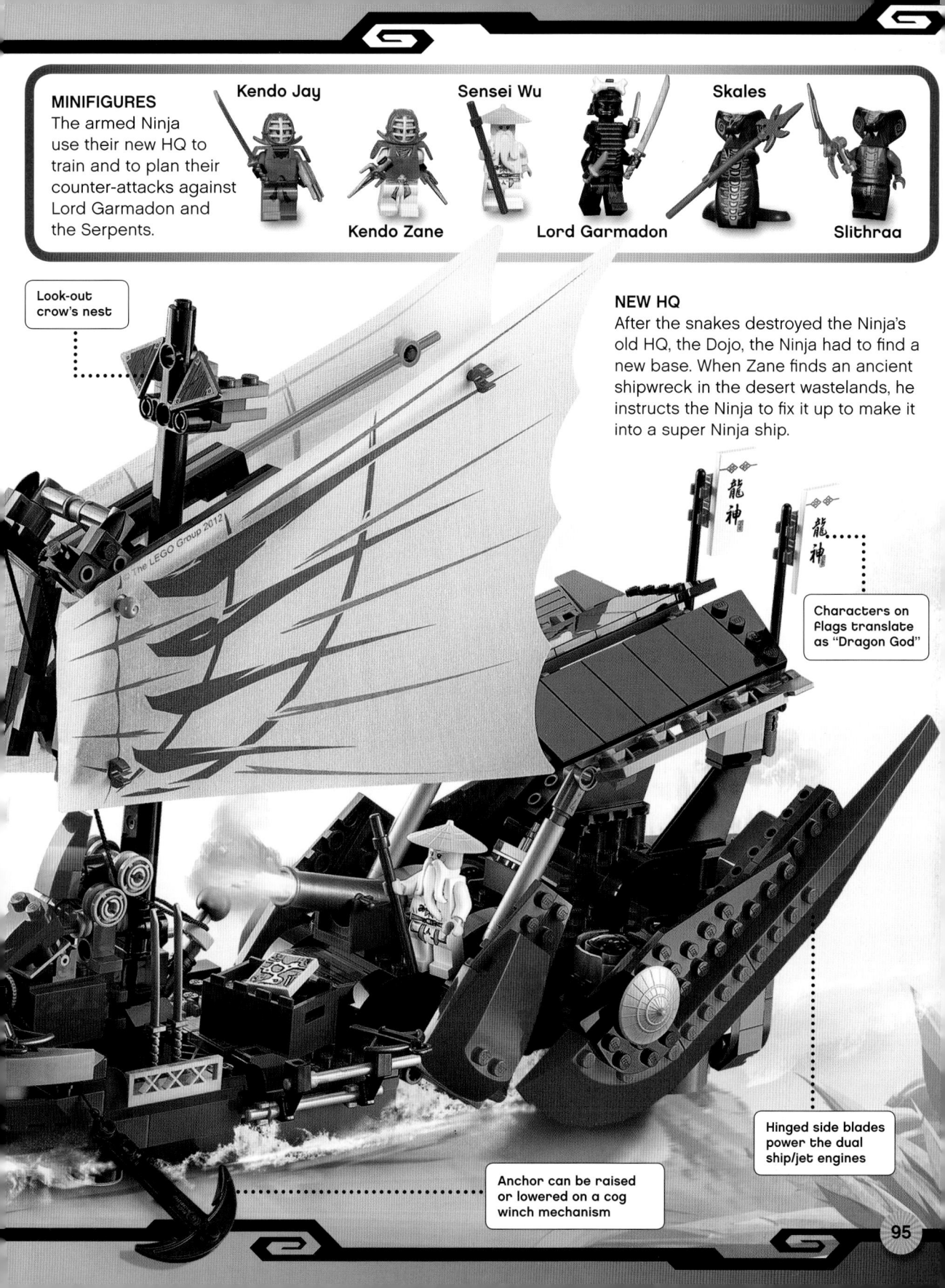

MINIFIGURES
The armed Ninja use their new HQ to train and to plan their counter-attacks against Lord Garmadon and the Serpents.

NEW HQ
After the snakes destroyed the Ninja's old HQ, the Dojo, the Ninja had to find a new base. When Zane finds an ancient shipwreck in the desert wastelands, he instructs the Ninja to fix it up to make it into a super Ninja ship.

KAI ZX

FIRE ZEN EXTREME

SINCE BATTLING THE Skeleton Army, Kai has worked hard to achieve the next level of his Ninja training—ZX, or Zen eXtreme level. His ZX minifigure is ready to take on new challenges and enemies.

NINJA FILE

SET NAME Kai ZX

SET NUMBER 9561

YEAR 2012

PIECES 21

ZX hood features golden helmet crown

Gold shoulder pauldrons

Protective chest plate over simple red tunic

Throwing stars tucked into belt

WEAPONS

DRAGON SWORD OF FIRE
This unique weapon gives its wielder the power of Fire!

Ancient, ornate blade

SILVER SERPENT STRIKER
This pronged weapon is useful when battling the deadly snakes.

BO STAFF
This fighting staff can be used for blocks, strikes, and sweeps at an enemy.

Simple wooden staff

ZX MINIFIGURE
Kai's ZX robes are printed with protective armor, weapons, and two red belts that secure everything in place during battle.

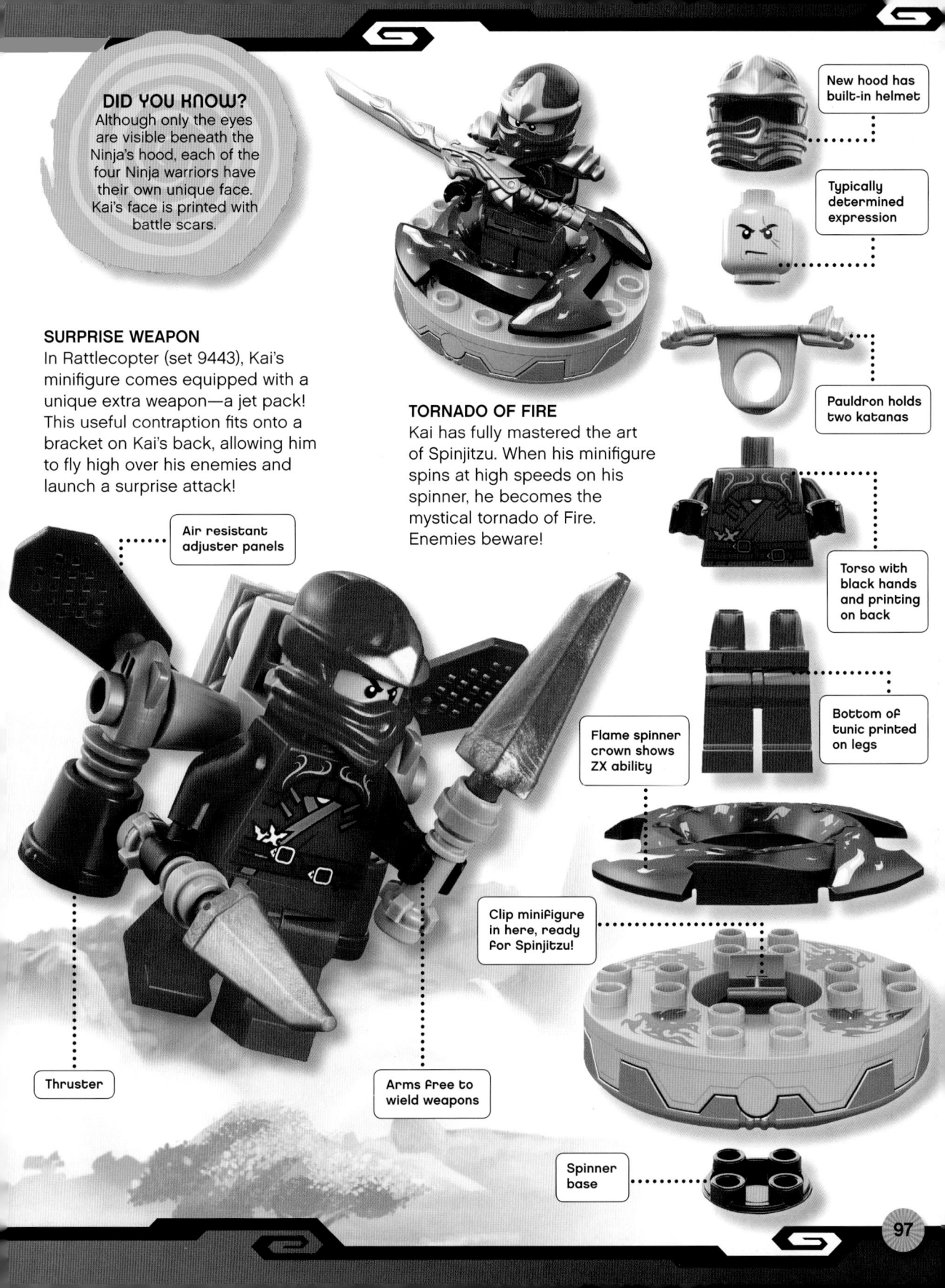

DID YOU KNOW?

Although only the eyes are visible beneath the Ninja's hood, each of the four Ninja warriors have their own unique face. Kai's face is printed with battle scars.

SURPRISE WEAPON

In Rattlecopter (set 9443), Kai's minifigure comes equipped with a unique extra weapon—a jet pack! This useful contraption fits onto a bracket on Kai's back, allowing him to fly high over his enemies and launch a surprise attack!

TORNADO OF FIRE

Kai has fully mastered the art of Spinjitzu. When his minifigure spins at high speeds on his spinner, he becomes the mystical tornado of Fire. Enemies beware!

BLADE CYCLE

BATTLE OF THE BLADES

THIS FIERY VEHICLE is Kai's sleek and speedy Serpent-battling machine. The two-wheeler is perfect for chasing after sneaky snakes, such as Rattla. At the touch of a button, the sides flip out to reveal deadly blades, which are perfect for knocking over enemies.

NINJA FILE

SET NAME KAI'S BLADE CYCLE

SET NUMBER 9441

YEAR 2012

PIECES 188

DEADLY BLADES
Press down on the red brick in front of the handlebars to flick out two large red side pieces, with golden blades underneath. Use the yellow pointed bricks to clip the blades into place. Watch out, Rattla!

MINIFIGURES
Can Kai defeat the mind-controlling Serpent, Rattla, with his Blade Cycle's big blade attack? He must retrieve the Hypnobrai Staff and its precious anti-venom.

IN ACTION!
Rattla has stolen the Hypnobrai Staff and its anti-venom, so Kai gives chase on his Blade Cycle. Will he be able to catch the slippery Serpent and knock him down with the side-projecting battle blades?

JAY ZX

LIGHTNING ZEN EXTREME

JAY HAS LEARNED many new skills from his teacher and master, Sensei Wu. His dedication to learning the ancient martial arts has certainly earned Jay his ZX Ninja status. This agile warrior is always ready to use his skills in the battle to save the world of Ninjago.

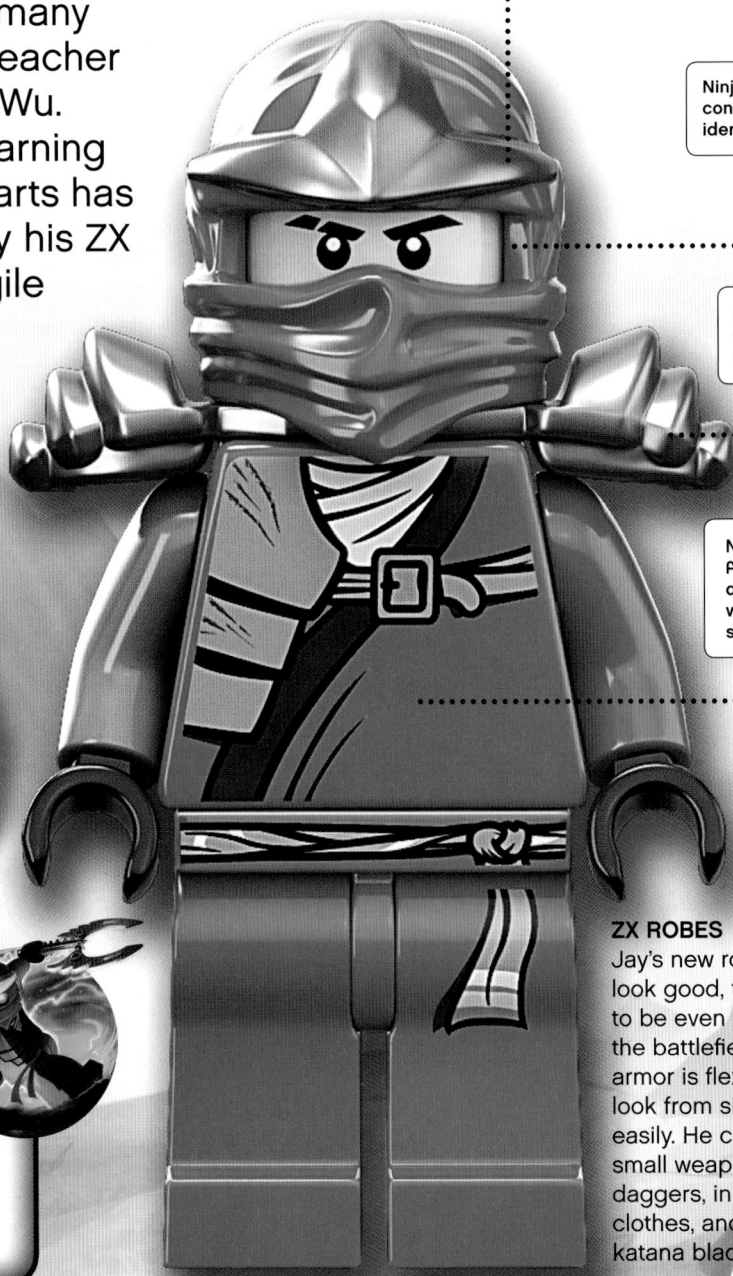

DID YOU KNOW?
Jay has a secret crush on Nya. When he cuts himself on a Fangpyre fossil skeleton and starts to turn into a snake, a kiss from Nya cures him and allows him to reach his full Ninja potential.

NINJA FILE

SET NAME JAY ZX
SET NUMBER 9553
YEAR 2012
PIECES 28

ZX ROBES
Jay's new robes don't just look good, they help him to be even more agile on the battlefield. The light armor is flexible, so he can look from side to side easily. He can also hide small weapons, such as daggers, in the folds of his clothes, and carry two katana blades on his back.

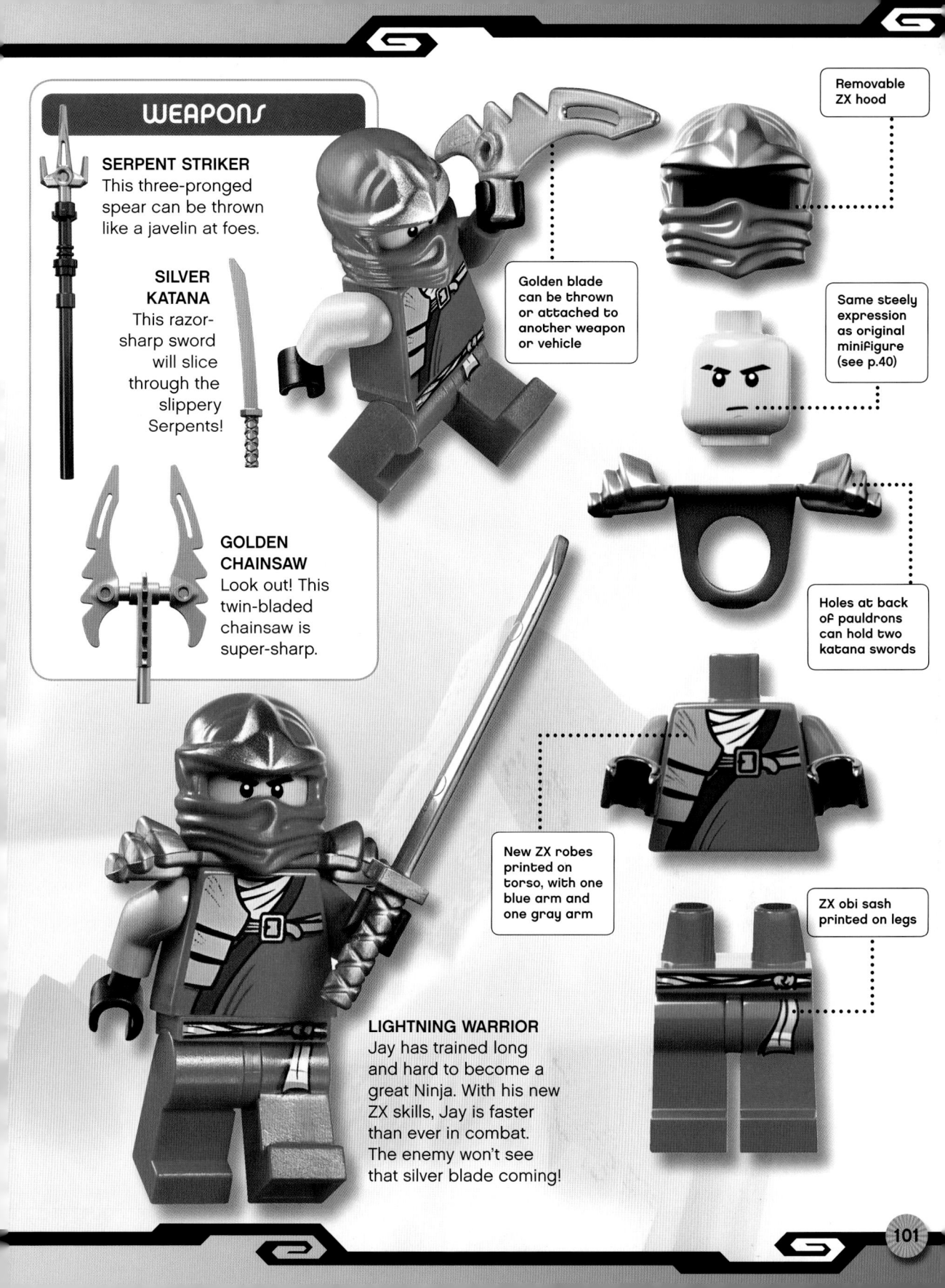
WEAPONS
SERPENT STRIKER
This three-pronged spear can be thrown like a javelin at foes.
SILVER KATANA
This razor-sharp sword will slice through the slippery Serpents!
GOLDEN CHAINSAW
Look out! This twin-bladed chainsaw is super-sharp.
Removable ZX hood
Golden blade can be thrown or attached to another weapon or vehicle
Same steely expression as original minifigure (see p.40)
Holes at back of pauldrons can hold two katana swords
New ZX robes printed on torso, with one blue arm and one gray arm
ZX obi sash printed on legs
LIGHTNING WARRIOR
Jay has trained long and hard to become a great Ninja. With his new ZX skills, Jay is faster than ever in combat. The enemy won't see that silver blade coming!

STORM FIGHTER

FIGHTING WITH LIGHTNING

THE STORM FIGHTER is Jay's super-speedy, streamlined battle jet. He can blast through the skies at top speed and then "transform" the jet to launch the Storm's wing attack function, knocking his enemies flying in all directions. Watch out, Serpents!

NINJA FILE

SET NAME JAY'S STORM FIGHTER

SET NUMBER 9442

YEAR 2012

PIECES 242

NINJA PILOT
Jay is a skilled pilot and loves flying his jet. He is deadly fast in combat on the ground and in the sky he strikes out of the blue, just like his elemental power—Lightning. Jay's enemies are often caught by surprise.

Cockpit lid lifts up

Streamlined jet nose piece

Golden serrated blade

IN THE COCKPIT
The tinted plastic cockpit lid opens and closes to allow Jay's minifigure to be slotted into position in the pilot seat of his Storm Fighter.

MINIFIGURES
Jay must recover the Golden Fangpyre Staff and its powerful anti-venom. Snappa is not going to give it up without a fight.

Jay ZX

Snappa

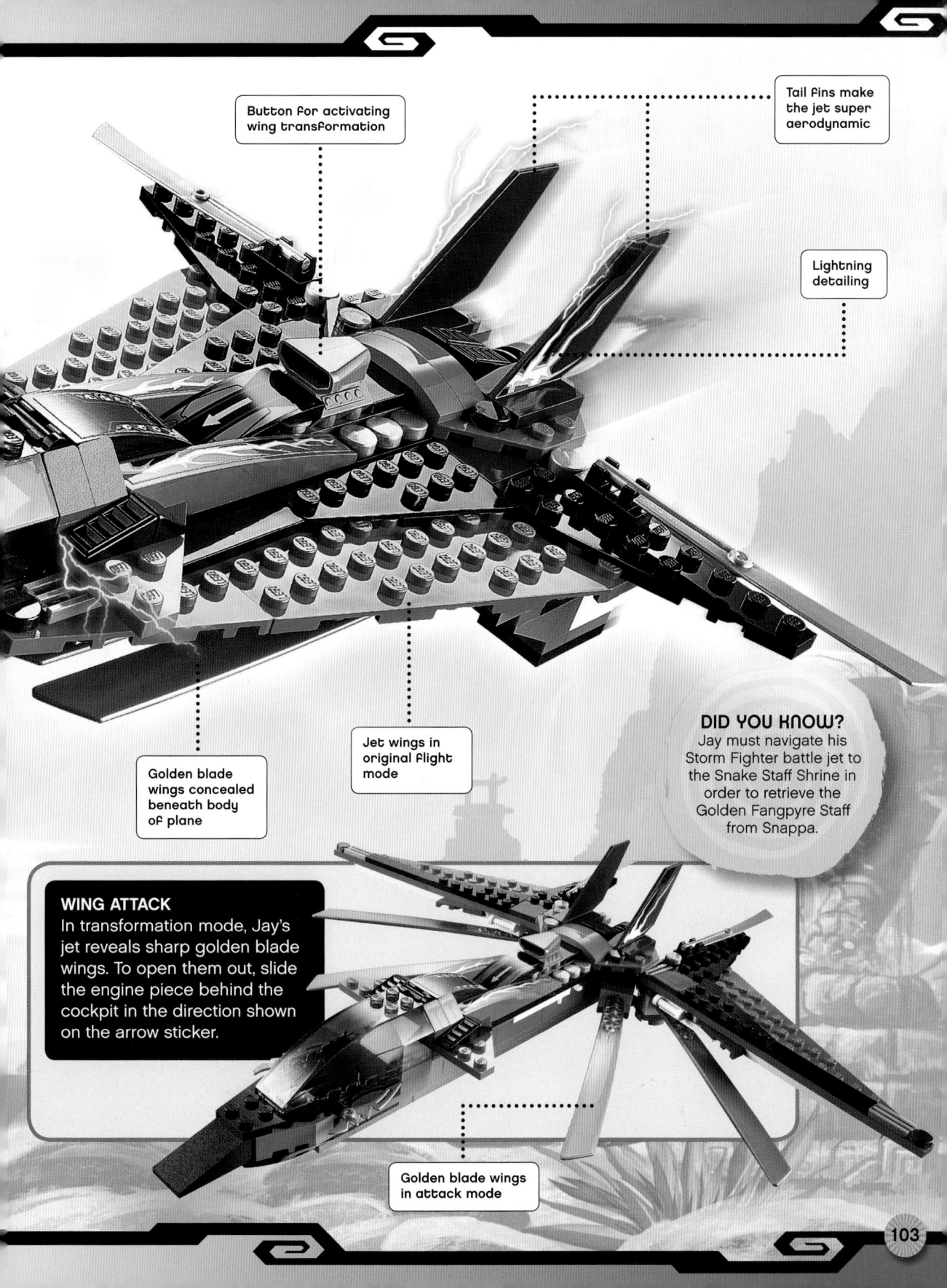

DID YOU KNOW?
Jay must navigate his Storm Fighter battle jet to the Snake Staff Shrine in order to retrieve the Golden Fangpyre Staff from Snappa.

WING ATTACK
In transformation mode, Jay's jet reveals sharp golden blade wings. To open them out, slide the engine piece behind the cockpit in the direction shown on the arrow sticker.

SAMURAI X

SECRET WARRIOR

WHO IS HIDING behind Samurai X's mask? For a while no one knows who this mysterious secret warrior is, but one day the truth is revealed to Jay. Samurai X is Nya, Kai's sister! Kai told her that only a Ninja could fight villains. However, Nya shows him that a Samurai (and a girl!) has what it takes to be a hero!

DID YOU KNOW?
"Samurai" was the name given to ancient Japanese warriors. The Samurai's main weapon was the katana sword and warriors often gave their blades names.

NINJA FILE

SET NAME SAMURAI X
SET NUMBER 9566
YEAR 2012
PIECES 23

ONE OF THE BOYS
When Samurai X reveals her identity, the Ninja are surprised. However, they see that Nya is just as brave and skilled as they are. She might even be able to teach them some things!

SAMURAI SPINNER
Nya practices hard and is a skilled sword fighter. With her super Samurai spinner she can whip up a fierce and fiery tornado.

WEAPONS

BUTTERFLY SWORD
This weapon looks good and also helps Samurai X to fight against the Serpentine.

GOLDEN KATANA
The blade of this Samurai weapon is deadly sharp.

SPEAR OF FIRE
No one knows the true powers of Samurai X's special spear, not even Nya herself.

GIRL POWER!
Nya is smart, but the Ninja don't always listen to her. She is able to cure a Fangpyre bite and knows that getting just one Fang Blade will stop the Great Devourer being unleashed.

SAMURAI MECH

ROBOT WARS

THE SAMURAI MECH is a massive robot controlled by Samurai X. It comes equipped with a fierce arsenal of weapons—including a cannon shooter, a flick missile device, sharp claws for crushing, and a mighty sword—but will all this be enough to fend off the Serpents?

Bytar Snike Samurai X

MINIFIGURES
Rare minifigures Bytar and Snike don't stand much of a chance against the might of Samurai X's Mech.

Samurai Mech helmet in raised position

Samurai X (aka Nya)

Bytar and Snike held captive in grabber claw

ROBO-POWERED
The Mech's helmet lifts up to reveal Samurai X's cockpit. Its giant hands have grabber claws that open and close for grasping weapons or even minifigures.

CATAPULT AMBUSH
Snike and Bytar have a catapult to launch missiles—or themselves—at Samurai X! Flick the rod piece to launch chaos from the barrel.

Serpent catapult mechanism

DID YOU KNOW?
The Snike minifigure is exclusive to Samurai Mech, (set 9448), whereas Samurai X and Bytar also appear in their own spinner sets. This is the only non-spinner set to include none of the four Ninja.

ROBOT MIGHT
Samurai X, aka Nya, has adorned her powerful Mech robot with Samurai detailing to intimidate her enemies. As she maneuvers the Mech to grab the Constrictai Fang Blade, Bytar and Snike launch a catapult ambush on her and the robot.

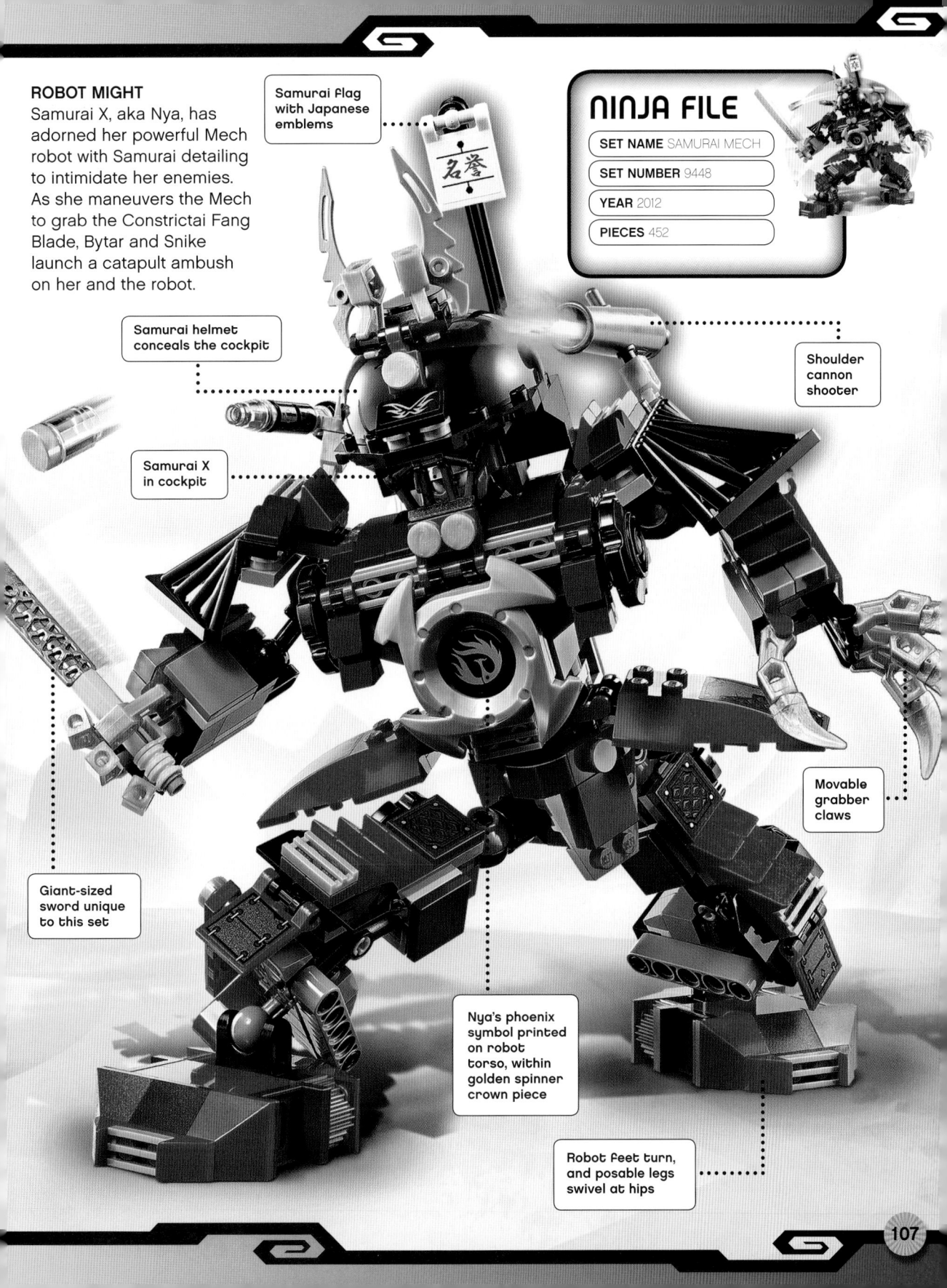

NINJA FILE

SET NAME SAMURAI MECH
SET NUMBER 9448
YEAR 2012
PIECES 452

COLE ZX

EARTH ZEN EXTREME

THANKS TO HOURS of practice, Cole has achieved the ZX, or Zen, level of his Ninja training. The Cole ZX minifigure wears a new uniform to mark his raised status. As leader of the Ninja, it is now Cole's job to help the others develop their own Zen eXtreme skills.

New hood has silver detail

NINJA FILE

SET NAME STARTER SET

SET NUMBER 9579

YEAR 2012

PIECES 62

Ninja wrap masks face

Protective leather-style chest plate

ZX black robe, chest sash, and belt printed on torso and legs

WEAPONS

TRUSTY AX
This ax is the perfect defensive weapon. The silver color matches Cole's pauldrons.

NINJAGO SWORD
Cole's sword skills are even better now he has achieved his Zen status.

Pointed striker head

GOLDEN TRI SCYTHE
This three-pronged weapon is the ultimate Serpentine repellent.

ZX UNIFORM
As a ZX Ninja, Cole wears silver shoulder pauldrons to protect his upper body. The back of the pauldrons form a circular holder, where Cole keeps his katana sword.

ZX SPINNER
Cole's super new ZX spinner features swinging chain attachments for even more Spinjitzu power. Protective side barriers also keep Cole safe while he spins.

HYPNOBRAI WEAPONS
ZX Cole battles with the Hypnobrai Serpents to retrieve the Hypnobrai Staff with its precious anti-venom. He also snatches the Scythe of Quakes.

TREAD ASSAULT

SERPENTS BEWARE!

THIS FOUR-WHEELED vehicle is tough enough to take on the evil leader of the Hypnobrai tribe, General Skales! Driven by Cole, it is armed with a rocket missile launcher and six terrifying Ninja blades. It also has a secret camouflage mode for surprise attacks. Watch out, General Skales, Cole is coming to get you!

NINJA FILE

SET NAME COLE'S TREAD ASSAULT

SET NUMBER 9444

YEAR 2012

PIECES 286

SLIPPERY ENEMY
Cole hopes that this powerful assault vehicle will help him defeat General Skales and reclaim the Hypnobrai Staff. However, Skales has a few tricks of his own, including some evil mind control powers.

Rocket missile can be fired at enemies.

Rocket shooter

Two golden katana swords at front of vehicle

Two golden daggers provide extra piercing action.

MINIFIGURES
Cole must stop Skales escaping with the Hypnobrai Staff. Luckily, his assault vehicle is fast!

Skales

Cole ZX

SNAKE DISGUISE
Cole's Tread Assault vehicle has a clever camouflage device for sneaking into Serpentine territory. When it is flipped over, green Serpentine-styling is revealed—Cole can even drive it in this position!

ZANE ZX

ICE ZEN EXTREME

ZANE IS NOW an expert ZX, or Zen eXtreme, Ninja. His ZX minifigure features gold pauldrons and gold detailing on his hood to reflect his new status. Zane's mastery of the Element of Ice has also reached an even higher level.

NINJA FILE

SET NAME ZANE ZX

SET NUMBER 9554

YEAR 2012

PIECES 37

New hood has built-in crown

Katana sword fits into circular holder on back

Ridged gold shoulder pauldrons

New robes feature entwined rope belts and plain white undershirt

TWO KATANA
Zane is a stealthy Ninja and a brave warrior. Thanks to his new ZX outfit, he can carry two katana swords on his back. This means he can fight more than one Serpent at once. NINJA-GO!

DID YOU KNOW?
Zane is a robot. His father, Dr. Julien, turned Zane's memory switch (located in a hidden panel in his chest) off, so that Zane wouldn't know he was a robot and could therefore lead a normal life.

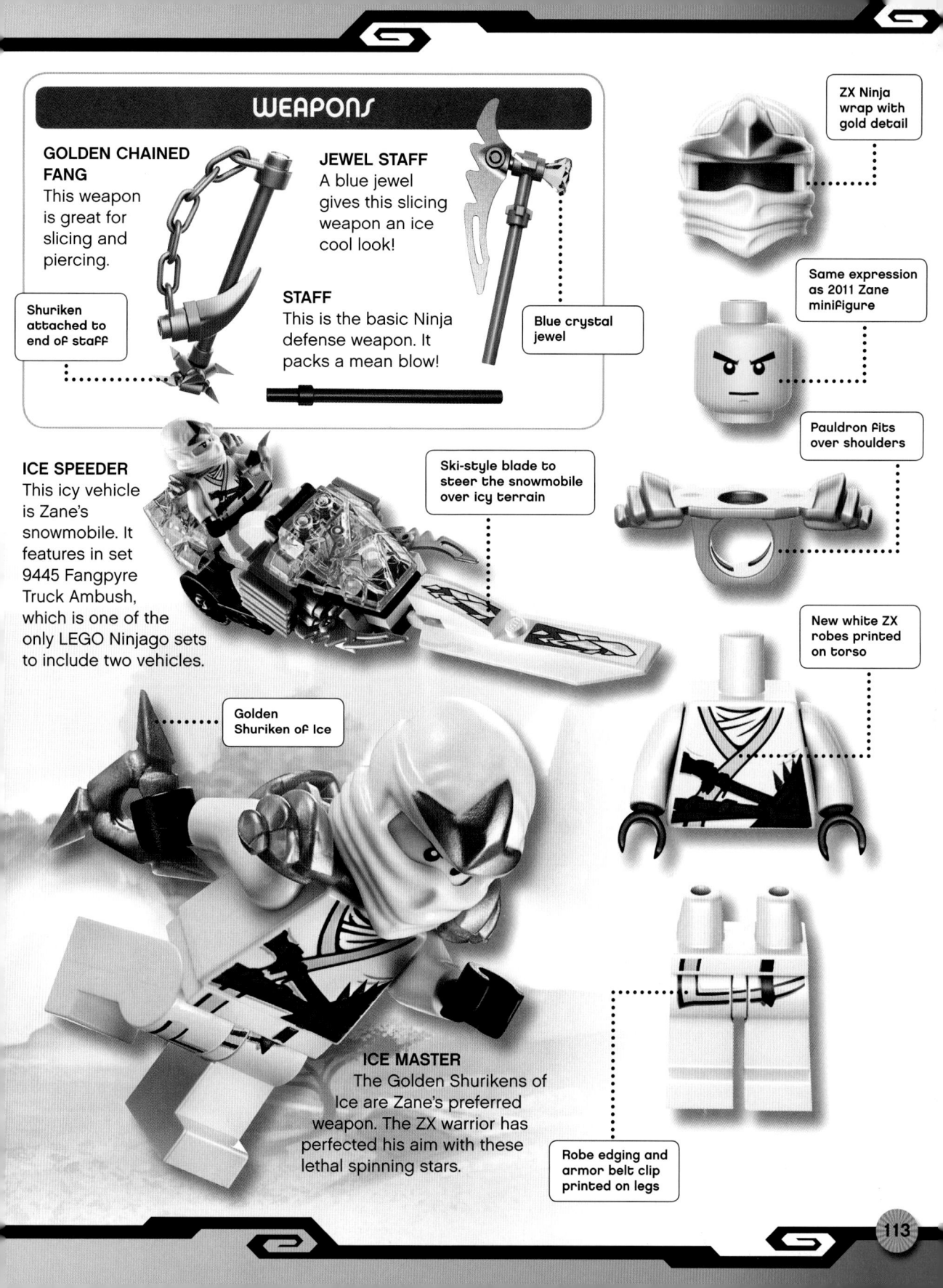
WEAPONS
GOLDEN CHAINED FANG
This weapon is great for slicing and piercing.
JEWEL STAFF
A blue jewel gives this slicing weapon an ice cool look!
STAFF
This is the basic Ninja defense weapon. It packs a mean blow!
Shuriken attached to end of staff
Blue crystal jewel
ZX Ninja wrap with gold detail
Same expression as 2011 Zane minifigure
Pauldron fits over shoulders
ICE SPEEDER
This icy vehicle is Zane's snowmobile. It features in set 9445 Fangpyre Truck Ambush, which is one of the only LEGO Ninjago sets to include two vehicles.
Ski-style blade to steer the snowmobile over icy terrain
New white ZX robes printed on torso
Golden Shuriken of Ice
ICE MASTER
The Golden Shurikens of Ice are Zane's preferred weapon. The ZX warrior has perfected his aim with these lethal spinning stars.
Robe edging and armor belt clip printed on legs

ULTRA SONIC RAIDER

TORNADO OF CREATION

THIS AWESOME SONIC vehicle is made from recycled scrap vehicles. It was created when the four Ninja used Spinjitzu to combine their four elemental tornadoes into the Tornado of Creation. With its dual tank/aircraft modes and multiple weapon functions, the Raider is the ultimate multipurpose fighting machine!

NINJA FILE

SET NAME ULTRA SONIC RAIDER

SET NUMBER 9449

YEAR 2012

PIECES 622

Attachment rail for aircraft

ULTRA SONIC TANK
The Ultra Sonic Raider is dual-functional, and can function separately as a tank and an aircraft. A red-tipped gray lever at the back of the Raider clicks the aircraft on and off the tank part.

Two Serpent minifigures can be locked into the prison cage at the back of the Raider.

ULTRA SONIC AIRCRAFT
The back part of the Raider lifts off to become a solo-piloted aircraft. The six long golden blades that feature as weapons on the tank open out to become the wings of the aircraft.

Adjustable speaker cannon

MINIFIGURES
United for the first time in one set, the four Ninja must battle the snakes and travel to Ninjago City in the Raider to destroy the Great Devourer.

Each cockpit can hold one minifigure.

Flame pieces fit into spinner crown pieces attached to the side of the tank.

Large double wheel to help steer the tank

Golden blades become wings when the Raider is in aircraft mode

Golden Weapon of Spinjitzu

A row of 8 golden sai daggers slots on to each side of the front of the tank.

Dagger flick missile—one on each side of the tank

Unique brown tire treads

SACRED MUSIC
The Serpents and the Great Devourer can be controlled by sacred flute music. Zane installs recordings of this music into the speaker cannon on the Raider, as a secret weapon.

KENDO NINJA

THE NINJA ARE always ready to learn new skills to give them an edge over their enemies. When Sensei Wu teaches them the complex martial art called Kendo, they have to train very hard to master this Samurai style of fighting. To be Kendo Ninja they must reach a higher level of physical agility and mental control. Have they got what it takes? Of course they have!

KAI

Sword-fighting is an important part of Kendo. Fortunately, Kai is already an expert with his elemental Weapon, the Dragon Sword of Fire. Kendo is no problem for Kai!

COLE

Kendo can be a very dangerous style of fighting, so the Ninja must wear armor. Cole has a protective helmet, mask, and body armor.

ZANE

Zane is the Ninja of Ice, but in his Kendo outfit he looks more like an ice hockey player. Zane just thinks he looks cool...

JAY

Once they have mastered Kendo, the Ninja can use any weapons they like. Jay chooses the dark talons and a golden blade.

NRG NINJA

EACH TIME A Ninja reaches the next level he gains a new status and a stylish new outfit. First, they become DX (Dragon eXtreme), then ZX (Zen eXtreme), then Kendo, and finally, when they reach their full potential, they become NRG Ninja. Each individual Ninja's full potential means something different, but for every one of them it means finding out who they really are.

JAY

A kiss from Kai's sister Nya unlocks Jay's full potential. His NRG outfit features an eye-catching new Lightning design.

KAI

Kai is the last to become an NRG Ninja. To progress to the highest level Kai must finally learn to control his fiery temper.

ZANE

Zane is the first Ninja to realize his full potential. For him it means learning that he is really a robot, and accepting that fact.

COLE

Leader Cole is the third Ninja to find his full potential. His NRG outfit is much brighter than his other ones—it is black and pink!

THE GREEN NINJA

MASTER OF ALL ELEMENTS

AN ANCIENT PROPHECY foretold that a Green Ninja would rise above all other Ninja, to fight the darkness. And here he is! The Green Ninja possesses the power of the four main Elements—Earth, Lightning, Ice, and Fire.

NINJA FILE

SET NAME EPIC DRAGON BATTLE

SET NUMBER 9450

YEAR 2012

PIECES 915

Lloyd's identity is hidden by his green wrap.

Detachable protective shoulder and back armor

Pale shirt worn beneath special Green Ninja robe

Unique silver belt clasp

WEAPONS

SUPER BOLT
Only the Green Ninja has this golden weapon, with its unique green blades.

SILVER SWORD
All Ninja are skilled in the art of sword fighting. The katana is the best sword to use in combat.

NIN-JÔ STAFF
A simple but classic weapon, this staff is effective in the hands of a trained Ninja.

NOT-SO-BAD
The Green Ninja's identity is revealed to be Lloyd Garmadon. He is not such a bad boy after all! When he went near the four Golden Weapons, a green aura appeared around him and he became the Green Ninja.

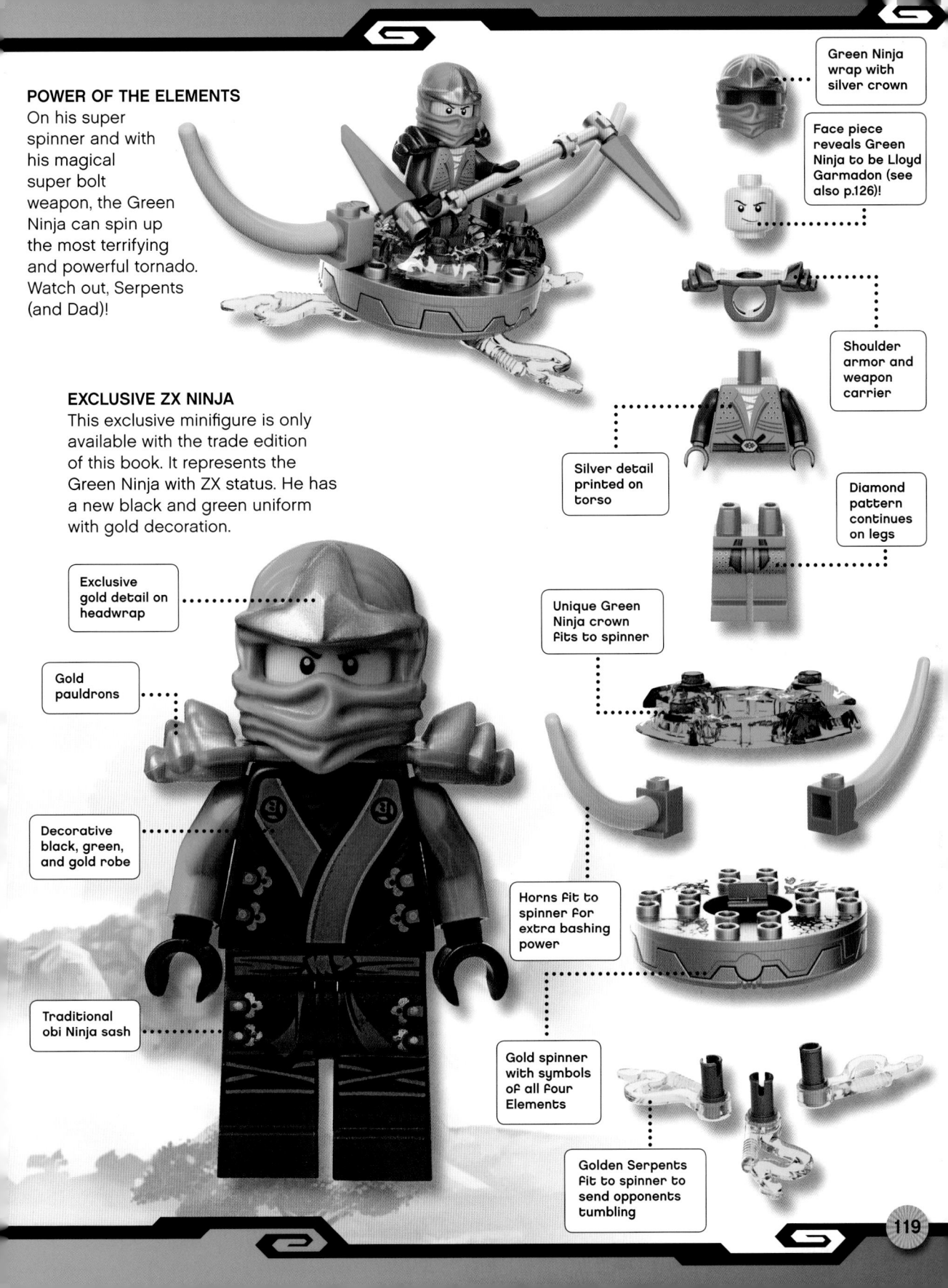

POWER OF THE ELEMENTS
On his super spinner and with his magical super bolt weapon, the Green Ninja can spin up the most terrifying and powerful tornado. Watch out, Serpents (and Dad)!

EXCLUSIVE ZX NINJA
This exclusive minifigure is only available with the trade edition of this book. It represents the Green Ninja with ZX status. He has a new black and green uniform with gold decoration.

MEET THE SERPENTINE

COME AND MEET the five Serpentine tribes—if you dare. Many years ago the Serpentine ruled Ninjago with the Great Devourer, but they were driven out and sealed into five separate tombs. Now, thanks to little Lloyd Garmadon, they're back! Each tribe has different markings, powers, and weapons, but they all have one thing in common—they are evil.

DID YOU KNOW?
The Hypnobrai, Fangpyre, Venomari, and Constrictai tribes each have their own Golden Staff. These weapons contain a vial of anti-venom —the only antidote to the Serpents' vile venom!

SNAKE TRIBES:

ANACONDRAI These purple snakes were the largest of the tribes, but only one remains. His jaws are big enough to swallow a person whole.

HYPNOBRAI These blue, cobra-like snakes have powerful, hypnotic eyes.

FANGPYRE These red Serpents turn their foes into snakes with one bite. They make vehicles for the other tribes.

VENOMARI A bite from these green four-eyed fiends causes victims to hallucinate (imagine things).

CONSTRICTAI These heavy orange and black Serpents live underground. They kill their enemies by crushing them.

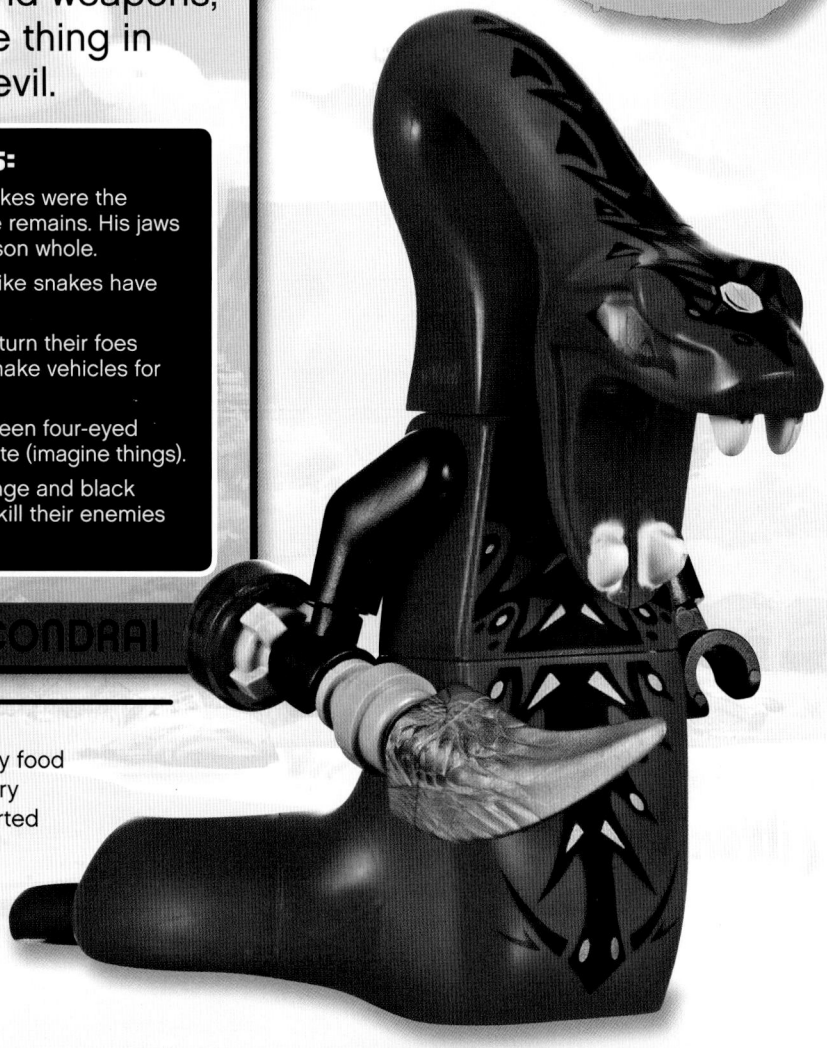

ANACONDRAI

PYTHOR

The Anacondrai didn't have any food in their tomb so they all got very hungry. Desperate, they all started eating each other until only General Pythor remained. He is now the supreme leader of all the Serpents. He is purple, poisonous, and perfectly horrible!

SKALES

General Skales is the leader of the Hypnobrai tribe but wants even more power! He is a master of the ancient martial art Fang-kwon-do.

MEZMO

This soldier is always happy to carry out General Skales's orders. Mezmo has the hypnotic red eyes and sharp fangs that are common to all Hypnobrai.

SLITHRAA

This warrior was his tribe's general, before Skales. Slithraa once tried to hypnotize Lloyd Garmadon but it backfired and he hypnotized himself instead!

RATTLA

Rattla is not the sharpest Serpent in the tribe, but he is happy to go along with whatever Skales tells him to do. He also has a secret passion for singing!

FANGPYRE

FANGDAM

Second-in-command of the Fangpyre tribe, Fangdam has two heads but can't speak from either of them.

SNAPPA

This fiery Fangpyre is his tribe's scout and sniper, which means he is great at finding—and catching—foes.

ACIDICUS

General Acidicus is the brains of the Venomari tribe—but that is not saying much! He makes sure that the tribe never runs out of venom.

FANG-SUEI

Fang-Suei is so strong and tough that he can use a banana as a weapon! Don't mess with this slippery Serpent.

FANGTOM

Two heads are definitely better than one for Fangpyre General Fangtom. His heads like to finish each other's sentences!

LASHA

Despite his missing eye, Lasha is the Venomari's chief scout. With his good eye, he has no problem spotting the enemy.

VENOMARI

LIZARU

This four-fanged Venomari is a fearsome warrior. He likes to help Acidicus plan their battles against the Ninja.

SPITTA

Spitta's teeth are so large that he can't close his mouth. That means all his venom leaks out and he can sell it to the other Venomari.

CONSTRICTAI

BYTAR

This Constrictai warrior has plenty of muscles, but not much height. His favorite things are fighting, eating, and sleeping.

SKALIDOR

General Skalidor isn't quite as fit and muscular as the rest of his tribe, but if anyone attacks him he can always sit on them!

SNIKE

Snike is the Constrictai's sniper. Unfortunately he is color-blind and cross-eyed! However, he still hits the target—most of the time.

CHOKUN

Chokun is pretty small for a Serpent. But what he lacks for in height and muscle, he makes up for in fang size.

THE NINJA ARE HISSSSTORY!

TO SLITHER LIKE A SERPENTINE YOU MUST:

MASTER YOUR TRIBE'S SPECIAL POWER

BE VICIOUS, CUNNING, AND SNEAKY

KEEP YOUR FANGS SHARPENED

ALWAYS OBEY YOUR GENERAL

LORD GARMADON

THE RETURN

HE'S BACK! HAVING returned from the Underworld, Lord Garmadon still wants to take over Ninjago, and also wants revenge on the Ninja for thwarting his evil plans. This time he is stronger than ever with a double torso and four arms! However, he is also a father, and his love for his son might just make him a better person...

NINJA FILE

SET NAME EPIC DRAGON BATTLE

SET NUMBER 9450

YEAR 2012

PIECES 915

DID YOU KNOW?

The new version of Garmadon's minifigure is made up of the same head and body as his 2011 minifigure (see p.50), with an extra upper body piece to hold two additional arms!

Nunchucks of Lightning

Sword of Fire

Scythe of Quakes

Removable second torso with two extra arms

Shuriken of Ice

FOUR ARMS
Thanks to his four arms, Lord Garmadon can now control all four Golden Weapons of Spinjitzu. He is a formidable opponent but he will help an enemy if it means saving his beloved son, Lloyd.

LLOYD GARMADON

SON OF LORD GARMADON

LLOYD IS NOT quite as bad as his father, Lord Garmadon. Young Lloyd attends Darkley's Boarding School for Bad Boys and is more interested in candy and practical jokes than plotting to take over Ninjago.

NINJA FILE

SET NAME LLOYD GARMADON

SET NUMBER 9552

YEAR 2012

PIECES 26

WEAPONS

SPEAR OF FORKED-TONGUES
Each tongue is filled with venom, ready to be injected into enemies.

GOLDEN VIPER
A small but lethal poisonous snake.

BLINDING STAFF
Shine the light in the enemies eyes to blind them.

SNAKE CHARMER
Lloyd accidentally releases all the Serpent tribes and becomes their leader. He orders the Serpents to do childish things such as steal candy. The snakes are not impressed and soon betray him. Fortunately, his Uncle Wu and the Ninja come to his rescue.

Black hooded cloak is removable

Cheeky expression

Sports-style top mixed with hand-painted skeleton design

Lloyd is still a child, so his minifigure has short, unposable legs.

VENOMARI SHRINE

SNAKE STAFF BATTLE

ZANE MUST USE his Ninja skills to retrieve the Golden Venomari Staff and the anti-venom hidden inside it. Can he avoid the snake fangs, slime, and acid spit in the Shrine and escape with the Staff?

NINJA FILE

SET NAME VENOMARI SHRINE

SET NUMBER 9440

YEAR 2012

PIECES 86

MINIFIGURES
Zane is attacked by poisonous vipers as he enters the Venomari Shrine alone. He must retrieve the Golden Staff with its anti-venom to save himself.

Zane ZX

Black plank viper launch pad

ATTACK!
Flick down the black tiled planks at the back of the Shrine to launch the poisonous green vipers. Watch them fly through the air towards the Ninja intruder!

Lime green snake venom

GOLDEN VENOMARI STAFF
The centerpiece of the Shrine is a large Serpent statue. Two long fangs filled with venom drip down to the floor and the Golden Staff hangs in front of them.

DID YOU KNOW?
The Venomari Staff is one of the four Serpent Staffs which are key elements in producing a map that will lead to the discovery of the four Fang Blades. Whoever has the four Fang Blades can unleash the Great Devourer.

TOXIC VENOM

The Venomari tribe's toxic venom causes terrible hallucinations in its victims. The General of the tribe, Acidicus, carries the Golden Venomari Staff, which contains a vial of anti-venom—the antidote to their own toxic venom!

ACIDICUS

VENOMARI GENERAL

NINJA FILE

SET NAME EPIC DRAGON BATTLE
SET NUMBER 9450
YEAR 2012
PIECES 915

Two rows of head spikes

Acidicus has two scars behind his left back eye.

Acidicus has two side fangs as well as two front fangs.

Distinctive green and orange scale pattern

Vial of anti-venom clips onto end of Hypnobrai Fang Blade handle

All Serpent Generals have a snake tail instead of legs.

GENERAL OF the Venomari Army, Acidicus is clever and crafty. He has constructed vials that the Venomari use to carry extra venom in their combat gear, so they never run out of poison in battle. How brilliantly evil!

FANG BLADES
Acidicus usually wields the Venomari Fang Blade, but here he's got the Hypnobrai one. There are four ancient silver Fang Blades for each of the four tribes (Venomari, Hypnobrai, Fangpyre, and Constrictai). Whoever holds all four Blades can unleash the Serpentine beast, the Great Devourer.

SPITTA

VENOMARI WARRIOR

THIS VENOMARI warrior's fangs are so large that his mouth is permanently open. Because of this, he drools a lot, leaking venom wherever he goes. Yuck—how slimy!

NINJA FILE

SET NAME SPITTA

SET NUMBER 9569

YEAR 2012

PIECES 20

Unique head markings

Four yellow eyes are a feature of all Venomari snakes.

Over-sized fangs, unique to Spitta

Light green scale pattern and scars printed on torso

Vials of venom carried in shoulder belt

WEAPONS

VENOM PICKAX
The venom vial makes this weapon even more lethal.

PURPLE VIPER
This purple snake is small but dangerous and highly toxic.

SCYTHE BLADE
This big, heavy, slicing blade is great for cutting down large enemies.

VENOM SUPPLIER
Spitta uses the vials invented by Acidicus to store his excess venom. He sells it to the other snakes in his tribe, for times when they can't produce enough venom of their own.

LASHA

VENOMARI SCOUT

LASHA IS THE best scout in the Venomari tribe, despite the fact that he has lost an eye. He keeps a lookout for enemies and seeks out prey for the rest of the Venomari to attack. Watch out, Ninja! Lasha is mean and isn't scared of anything.

NINJA FILE

SET NAME LASHA

SET NUMBER 9562

YEAR 2012

PIECES 21

Distinctive cobra hood, opened wide to intimidate enemies

Missing eye was lost in battle

Serpentine forked tongue

Bandolier shoulder belt for holding vials

Red vial for storing extra venom

WEAPONS

TOXIC VIPER
This tiny viper is highly poisonous and its bite causes hallucinations.

GOLDEN AX
The perfect Serpentine weapon. One swing will knock the enemy back.

Vial of venom

CHAINED FANG OF POISON
The green vial can be filled with venom and the piercing fang can be swung at the enemy.

SMALL FANGS
Lasha's fangs are too small to produce much venom of his own. He has to buy extra venom so that he has enough to use on his enemies. His fangs hurt most of the time because he ate too much candy when he was a young Serpent.

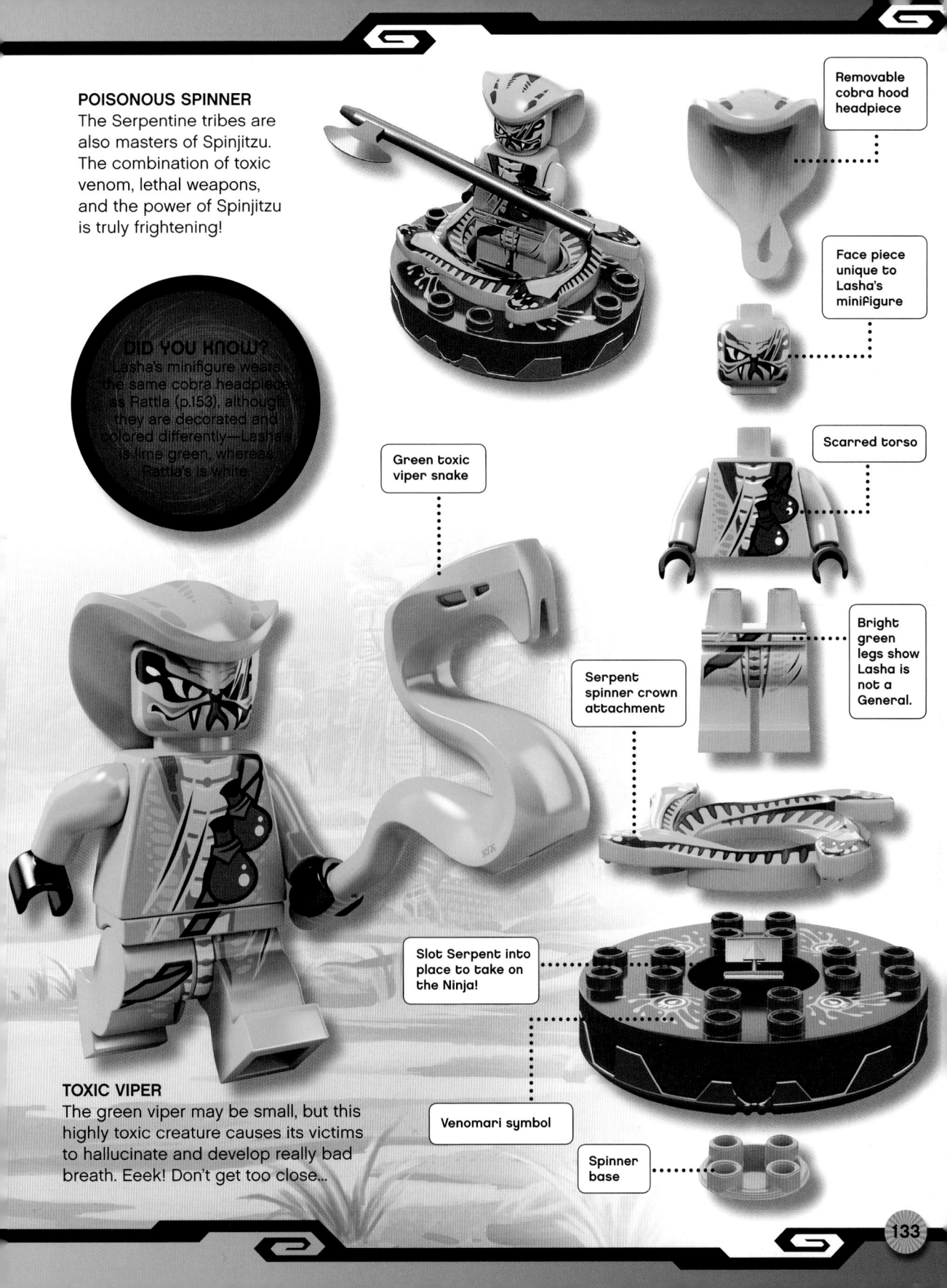

POISONOUS SPINNER
The Serpentine tribes are also masters of Spinjitzu. The combination of toxic venom, lethal weapons, and the power of Spinjitzu is truly frightening!

DID YOU KNOW?
Lasha's minifigure wears the same cobra headpiece as Rattla (p.153), although they are decorated and colored differently—Lasha's is lime green, whereas Rattla's is white.

TOXIC VIPER
The green viper may be small, but this highly toxic creature causes its victims to hallucinate and develop really bad breath. Eeek! Don't get too close...

LASHA'S BITE CYCLE

FANG BLADE THEFT

WHILE EXAMINING ONE of the long-lost Fang Blades in the Blacksmith's Forge, Cole is paid a surprise visit! Lasha zooms past on his slick Bite Cycle and seizes the Blade. Luckily for Lasha, the Bite Cycle is ideal for carrying out a stealth attack—it is lightning-fast, and the Serpent makes a quick getaway...

NINJA FILE

SET NAME LASHA'S BITE CYCLE

SET NUMBER 9447

YEAR 2012

PIECES 249

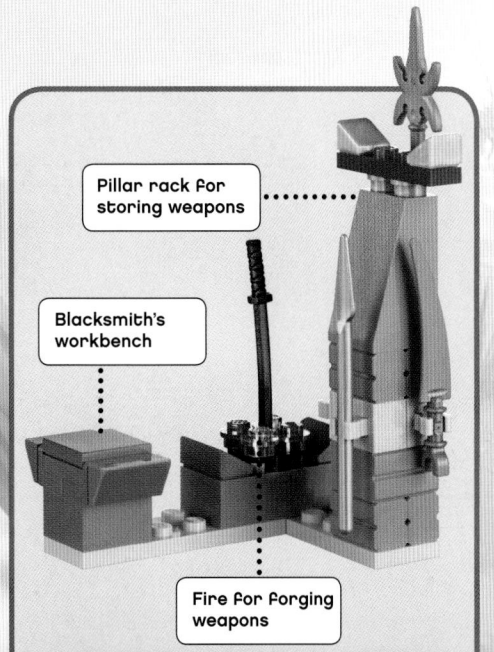

BLACKSMITH'S FORGE
This mini blacksmith's workshop features exclusively in this set and comes equipped with a forging fire, a workbench, a weapons rack, four regular weapons, and an anvil hammer.

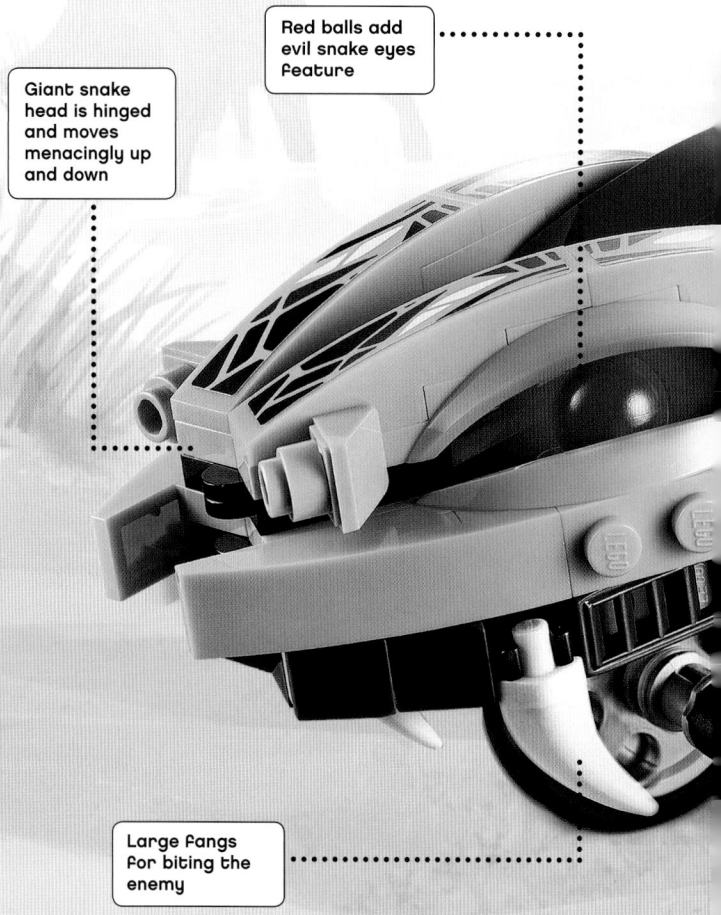

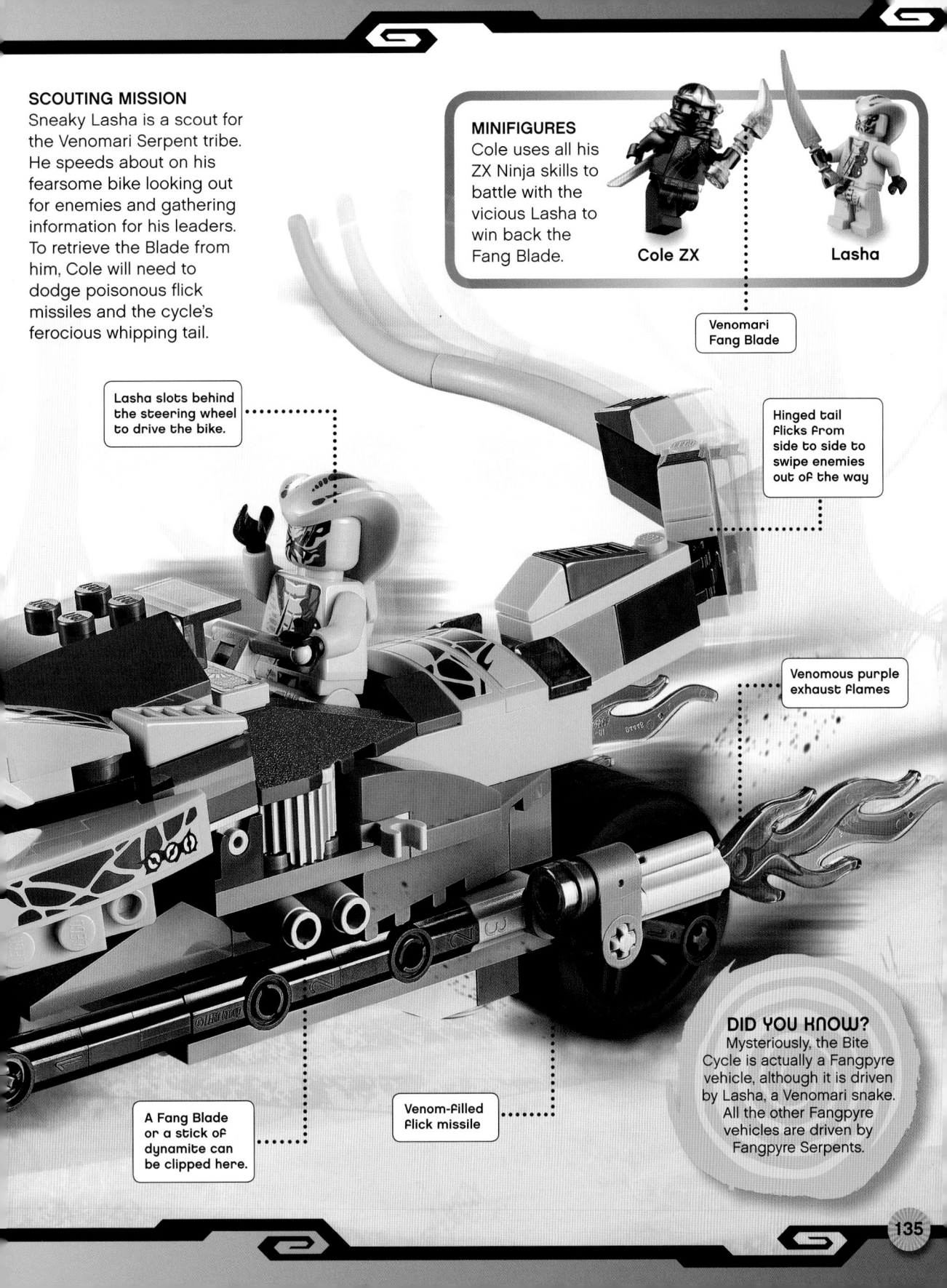

SCOUTING MISSION
Sneaky Lasha is a scout for the Venomari Serpent tribe. He speeds about on his fearsome bike looking out for enemies and gathering information for his leaders. To retrieve the Blade from him, Cole will need to dodge poisonous flick missiles and the cycle's ferocious whipping tail.

MINIFIGURES
Cole uses all his ZX Ninja skills to battle with the vicious Lasha to win back the Fang Blade.

Cole ZX

Lasha

DID YOU KNOW?
Mysteriously, the Bite Cycle is actually a Fangpyre vehicle, although it is driven by Lasha, a Venomari snake. All the other Fangpyre vehicles are driven by Fangpyre Serpents.

LIZARU

VENOMARI WARRIOR

THIS FOUR-FANGED warrior is second-in-command to Acidicus in the Venomari tribe. In his spare time he runs a potion-making business, to make lethal venoms for the Serpents.

NINJA FILE

SET NAME LIZARU

SET NUMBER 9557

YEAR 2012

PIECES 25

WEAPONS

AX
Simple and hefty, this ax is ideal for hacking through enemy troops.

BATTLE MACE
This swinging spiked ball could knock a minifigure into seven pieces!

DOUBLE-SIDED AX
This weapon has a fierce, double slicing action.

Distinctive striped head markings

Two rows of head spikes

Sinister yellow eyes

Four fangs filled with venom

Scaly, scarred torso similar to other members of the Venomari tribe

SCHEMING SERPENT
Lizaru can survive days or even weeks without food. He doesn't mind—it gives him time to think up terrifying schemes and make evil battle plans.

FANGTOM

FANGPYRE GENERAL

THIS TWO-HEADED snake is the General of the Fangpyre Tribe Army. Like all the Serpent Generals, Fangtom has a tail instead of legs. He is the brains of the tribe—two heads mean double the trouble for Ninja!

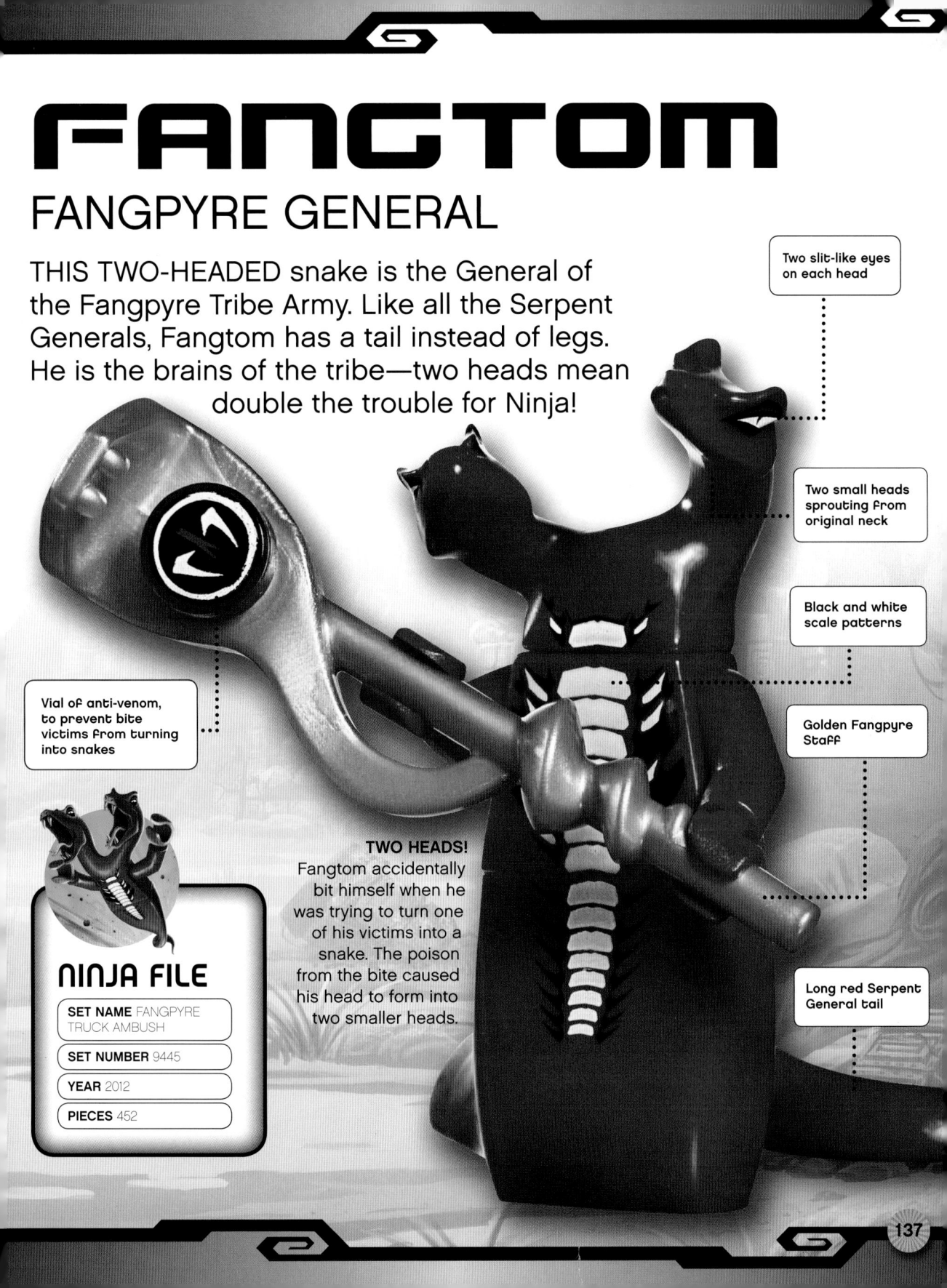

TWO HEADS! Fangtom accidentally bit himself when he was trying to turn one of his victims into a snake. The poison from the bite caused his head to form into two smaller heads.

NINJA FILE

SET NAME FANGPYRE TRUCK AMBUSH

SET NUMBER 9445

YEAR 2012

PIECES 452

FANGDAM

FANGPYRE WARRIOR

FANGDAM IS A warrior and second-in-command of the Fangpyre tribe. Fellow Serpent Fang-Suei once mistook him for a desert slug and bit him. The bite made him grow another head. Fangdam is fast, ferocious, and looks familiar...

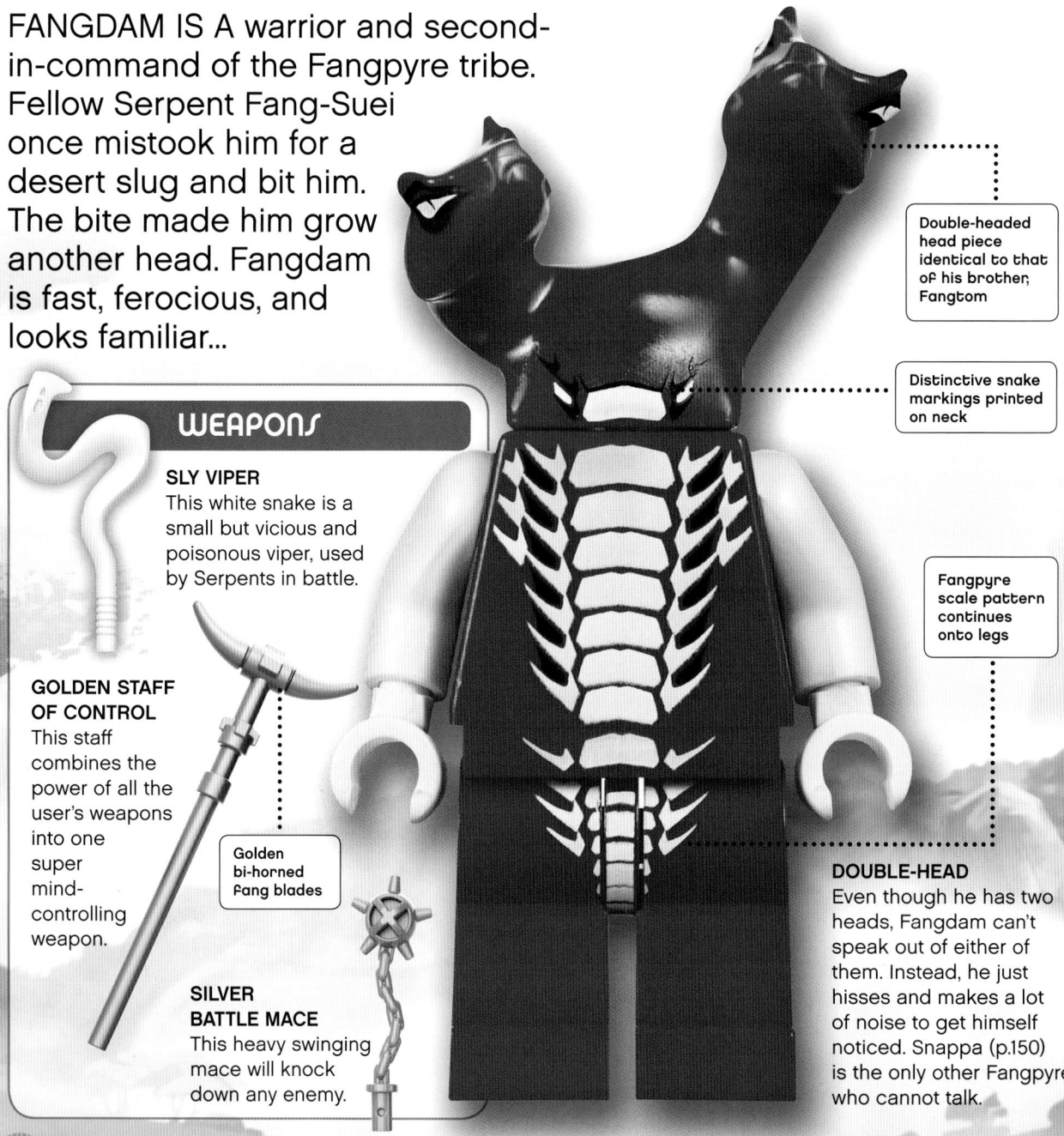

WEAPONS

SLY VIPER
This white snake is a small but vicious and poisonous viper, used by Serpents in battle.

GOLDEN STAFF OF CONTROL
This staff combines the power of all the user's weapons into one super mind-controlling weapon.

SILVER BATTLE MACE
This heavy swinging mace will knock down any enemy.

DOUBLE-HEAD
Even though he has two heads, Fangdam can't speak out of either of them. Instead, he just hisses and makes a lot of noise to get himself noticed. Snappa (p.150) is the only other Fangpyre who cannot talk.

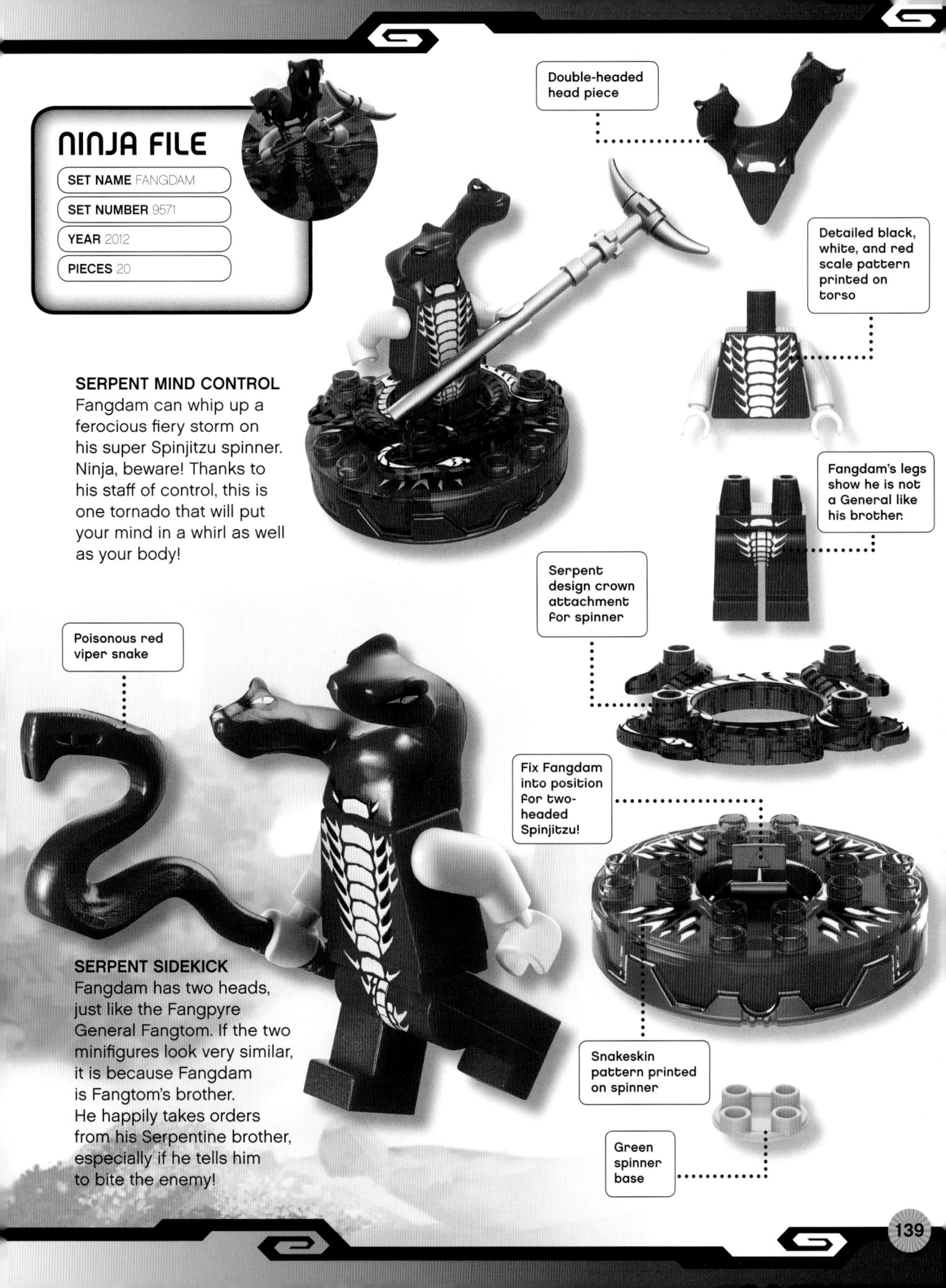
NINJA FILE
SET NAME FANGDAM
SET NUMBER 9571
YEAR 2012
PIECES 20
Double-headed head piece
Detailed black, white, and red scale pattern printed on torso
Fangdam's legs show he is not a General like his brother.
Serpent design crown attachment for spinner
Poisonous red viper snake
Fix Fangdam into position for two-headed Spinjitzu!
Snakeskin pattern printed on spinner
Green spinner base
SERPENT MIND CONTROL
Fangdam can whip up a ferocious fiery storm on his super Spinjitzu spinner. Ninja, beware! Thanks to his staff of control, this is one tornado that will put your mind in a whirl as well as your body!
SERPENT SIDEKICK
Fangdam has two heads, just like the Fangpyre General Fangtom. If the two minifigures look very similar, it is because Fangdam is Fangtom's brother. He happily takes orders from his Serpentine brother, especially if he tells him to bite the enemy!

FANGPYRE TRUCK

SERPENT AMBUSH!

ZANE AND JAY have been ambushed by the slippery brothers Fangtom and Fangdam. The dangerous duo are driving their ferocious Fangpyre Truck, and its giant snake head—with opening and closing jaw—can eat Ninja if it catches them! Slot the minifigure inside the jaw and clamp it shut. Gulp! Bye, bye, Ninja!

NINJA FILE

SET NAME FANGPYRE TRUCK AMBUSH

SET NUMBER 9445

YEAR 2011

PIECES 452

TAIL END
The Fangpyre Truck's long, segmented tail can be whipped from side to side to knock over the enemy. Turn the black cog to get maximum whipping movement.

Jointed tail pieces link together

Poisonous exhaust flames

Oversized gas-fed tubing

Lethal pointed fangs

Forked tongue flicks up and down—ssssss!

Evil snake eyes made from two red balls

DINNERTIME!
The Ninja can't leave without the Fangpyre Staff and its precious anti-venom, but the Truck's whipping tail is stopping them from getting close. Can they out-run the Fangpyre Truck before its snapping fanged jaws eat them for dinner?

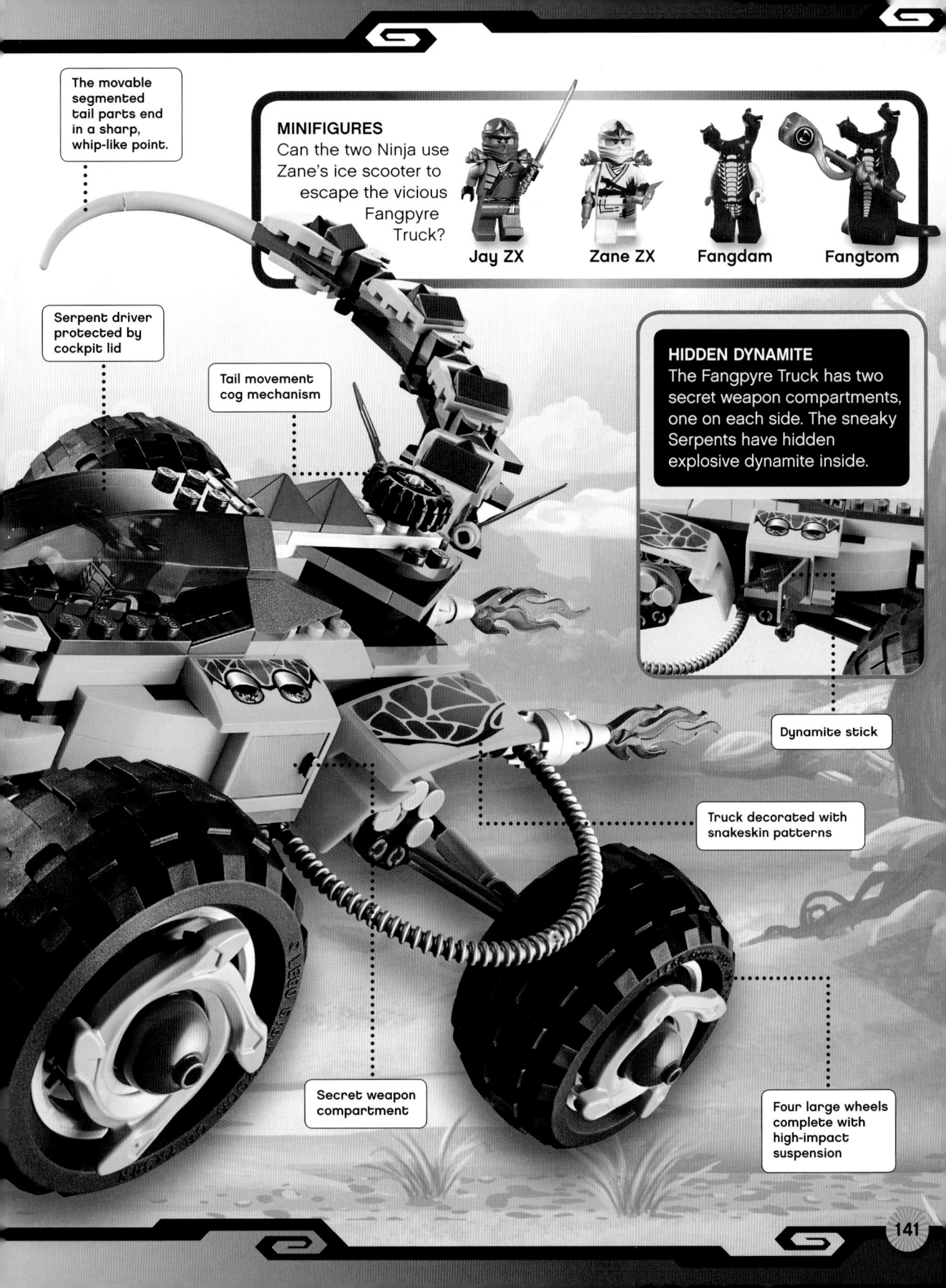
The movable segmented tail parts end in a sharp, whip-like point.
MINIFIGURES
Can the two Ninja use Zane's ice scooter to escape the vicious Fangpyre Truck?
Jay ZX
Zane ZX
Fangdam
Fangtom
Serpent driver protected by cockpit lid
Tail movement cog mechanism
HIDDEN DYNAMITE
The Fangpyre Truck has two secret weapon compartments, one on each side. The sneaky Serpents have hidden explosive dynamite inside.
Dynamite stick
Truck decorated with snakeskin patterns
Secret weapon compartment
Four large wheels complete with high-impact suspension

FANGPYRE WRECKING BALL

SNAKE TRICKS

LLOYD GARMADON TRIES to snatch the Fangpyre Staff, but the Serpents are one step ahead of him. To teach him a lesson, Fangdam activates the terrifying Fangpyre Wrecking Ball crane. Ninja to the rescue! Watch out for the swinging ball, biting jaws, and whipping tail.

NINJA FILE

SET NAME FANGPYRE WRECKING BALL

SET NUMBER 9457

YEAR 2012

PIECES 415

ARTICULATED ATTACK
The tail of the crane is jointed and fully articulated, so it can swing and bend in all directions. At the back of the crane there are two handy toolbox cabinets that can double up as a weapon store.

DID YOU KNOW?
When the Fangpyre snakes bite a vehicle, it gains snake-like abilities and a Serpentine appearance. The Fangpyre tribe provides most of the vehicles for the rest of the Serpent tribes.

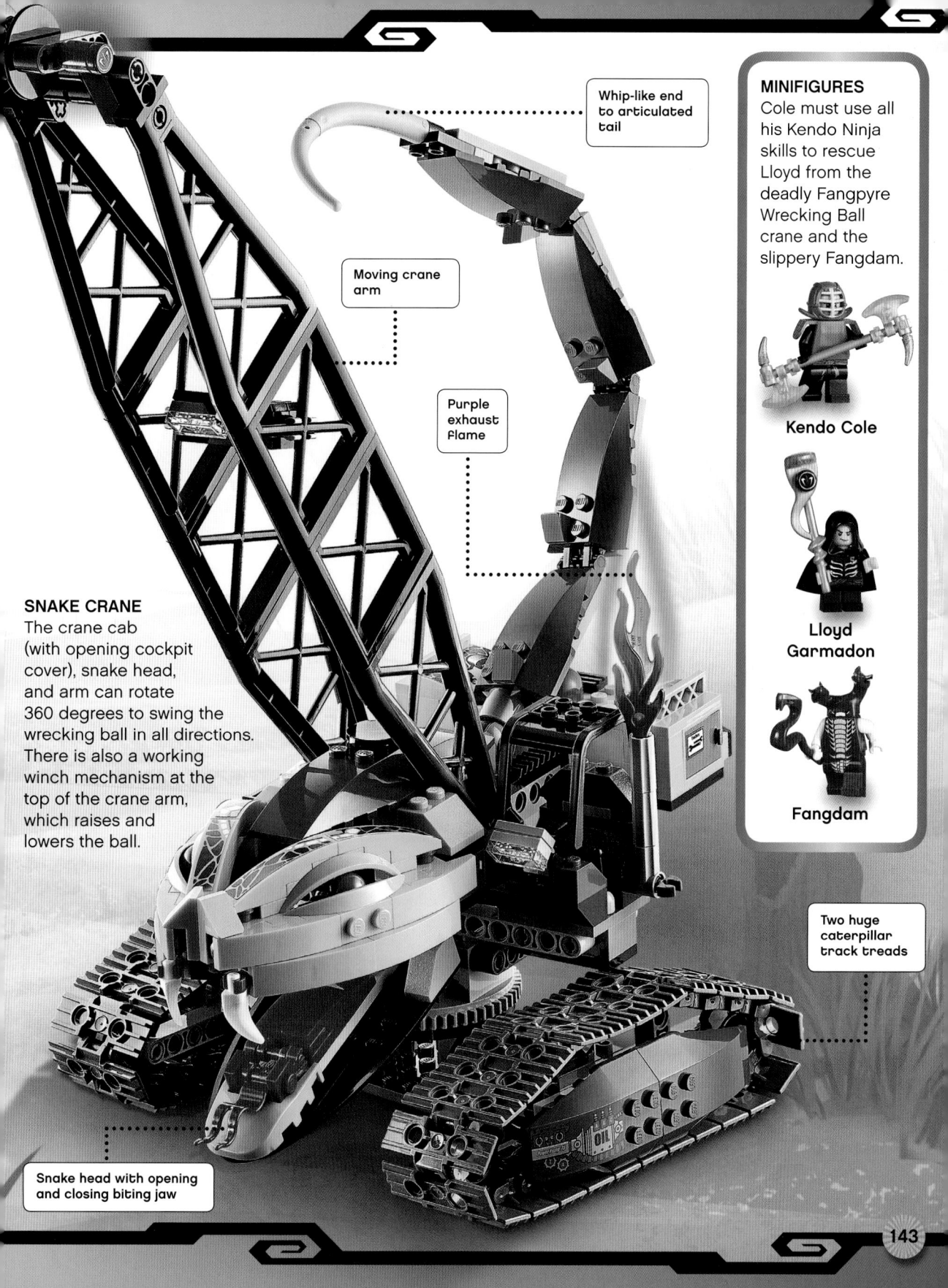

MINIFIGURES
Cole must use all his Kendo Ninja skills to rescue Lloyd from the deadly Fangpyre Wrecking Ball crane and the slippery Fangdam.

Kendo Cole

Lloyd Garmadon

Fangdam

SNAKE CRANE
The crane cab (with opening cockpit cover), snake head, and arm can rotate 360 degrees to swing the wrecking ball in all directions. There is also a working winch mechanism at the top of the crane arm, which raises and lowers the ball.

FANG-SUEI

FANGPYRE SOLDIER

FANG-SUEI IS the strongest of the Fangpyre soldiers and is quick to act on orders. He is always hungry and if he hasn't eaten, anyone who gets in his way is likely to become a tasty snack! He can turn people and machines into snakes with one deadly bite.

NINJA FILE

SET NAME FANG-SUEI

SET NUMBER 9567

YEAR 2012

PIECES 11

Unique snakeskin pattern on head

Distinctive narrow red head and long neck

Extra large poisonous fangs

Unique necklace made from fangs

DID YOU KNOW?
The Fangpyre are viper-like snakes. A poisonous bite from a Fangpyre can turn anything or anyone into a snake.

ACCIDENTAL BITE!
Hallucinating in the heat of a battle in a dry desert, Fang-Suei mistook Fangdam for the enemy and bit him. The poisonous bite caused Fangdam to grow a second head!

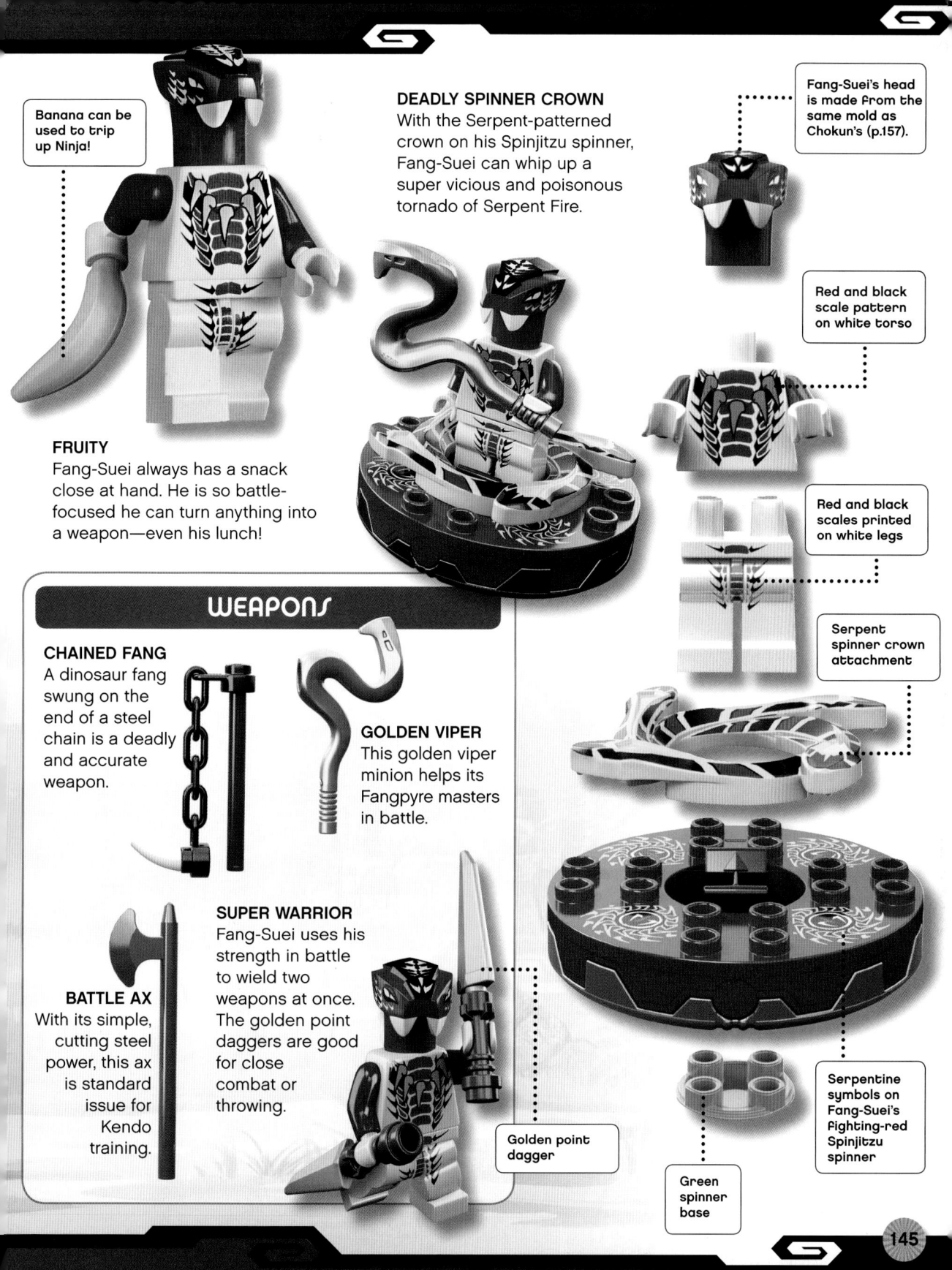
Banana can be used to trip up Ninja!
DEADLY SPINNER CROWN
With the Serpent-patterned crown on his Spinjitzu spinner, Fang-Suei can whip up a super vicious and poisonous tornado of Serpent Fire.
Fang-Suei's head is made from the same mold as Chokun's (p.157).
Red and black scale pattern on white torso
FRUITY
Fang-Suei always has a snack close at hand. He is so battle-focused he can turn anything into a weapon—even his lunch!
Red and black scales printed on white legs
WEAPONS
CHAINED FANG
A dinosaur fang swung on the end of a steel chain is a deadly and accurate weapon.
GOLDEN VIPER
This golden viper minion helps its Fangpyre masters in battle.
Serpent spinner crown attachment
BATTLE AX
With its simple, cutting steel power, this ax is standard issue for Kendo training.
SUPER WARRIOR
Fang-Suei uses his strength in battle to wield two weapons at once. The golden point daggers are good for close combat or throwing.
Golden point dagger
Serpentine symbols on Fang-Suei's fighting-red Spinjitzu spinner
Green spinner base

RATTLECOPTER

SKY WARS

WHO SAYS SNAKES can't fly? Fang-Suei corners Lloyd Garmadon with his mean, green, Ninja-fighting machine as the rebellious schoolboy tries to get away with the Constrictai Staff. The Rattlecopter poses a serious threat—Lloyd is in danger of being poisoned by lethal flick missiles or turned into a snake—unless Kai can come to his rescue...

SECRET SERPENT WEAPON
Fang-Suei's sly viper minions can be hidden in a cage at the back of the Rattlecopter. These poisonous snakes can then be dropped from the sky onto the enemy. Squeeze the two green side panels together at the point indicated by the arrows and launch Serpentine chaos!

BATTLE IN THE SKIES

This Serpent-themed helicopter is easy to fly. The rotating blades on top are specially angled down over the covered cockpit, so that you can hold the tail bar and maneuver the Rattlecopter to battle the enemies in the sky.

NINJA FILE

SET NAME RATTLECOPTER

SET NUMBER 9443

YEAR 2012

PIECES 327

Blades rotate 360 degrees for flying and hovering

Fang-Suei slots into the cockpit to pilot the Rattlecopter.

Dual flick missile launcher

Rotating tail blade can also be used as crown attachment for spinners

Hinged blades can be moved in and out during flight

Powerful thrusters

Fang-Suei's vicious viper minion

Snake-like Rattlecopter face includes two hanging hinged fangs

MINIFIGURES

Kai swoops in on his jet pack to snatch the Constrictai Staff and rescue Lloyd before Fang-Suei sinks his fangs into the young Garmadon.

Kai ZX

Fang-Suei

Lloyd Garmadon

FANGPYRE MECH

SERPENT POWER

THE FANGPYRE MECH is Fang-Suei's terrifying Serpent battle robot. This massive mechanical monster is armed with fangs, grabbing hands, and a poison missile launcher—and it does whatever Fang-Suei tells him to. Get ready Cole, the Fangpyres are coming to get you!

DID YOU KNOW?
The Mech and other Fangpyre vehicles were created when Fang-Suei and Kappa bit several ordinary broken-down vehicles.

Grabber hand can hold a minifigure

Kendo Cole spins up a super Earth tornado.

MINIFIGURES
Cole battles Fang-Suei's mighty Mech monster with the Scythe of Quakes. Fang-Suei is armed with a banana!

Fang-Suei

Kendo Cole

Missile contains a vial of venom

FIRE AT WILL!
Slot the poisonous flick missile into the hole on the Mech's right arm and flick away. The Fangpyre venom will turn its victim into a snake-like creature.

KENDO COLE
Cole has now achieved his Kendo Ninja status. With his advanced martial arts and weapon skills, will Cole be strong enough to defeat this powerful and dangerous Serpentine machine? The mean Mech might have met its match!

Flick missile slots into right arm
Fang-Suei pilots the Mech from a cockpit behind the snake head.
Snake tail can swing from side to side on a ball joint
Large sharp fangs
Head, arms, legs, and feet are attached to ball joints to make them flexible
Don't trip on the banana!
NINJA FILE
SET NAME FANGPYRE MECH
SET NUMBER 9455
YEAR 2012
PIECES 255

SNAPPA

FANGPYRE SCOUT

SNAPPA IS A scout and sniper in the Fangpyre tribe. He is a mean Serpent with a quick temper. Watch out—he usually bites first and worries about the consequences later. Of course, by then it is usually too late for his victims...

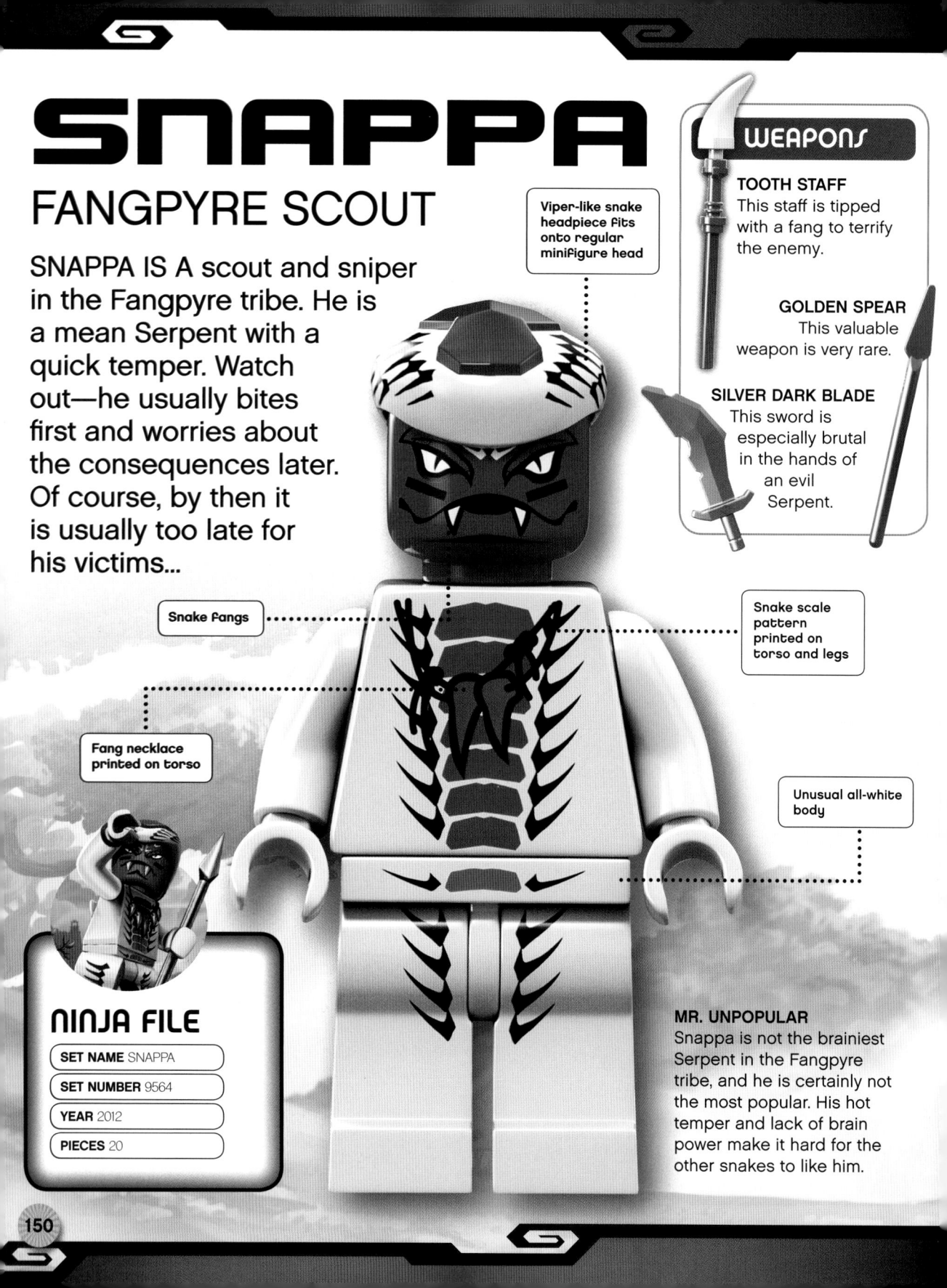

WEAPONS

TOOTH STAFF
This staff is tipped with a fang to terrify the enemy.

GOLDEN SPEAR
This valuable weapon is very rare.

SILVER DARK BLADE
This sword is especially brutal in the hands of an evil Serpent.

NINJA FILE

SET NAME SNAPPA
SET NUMBER 9564
YEAR 2012
PIECES 20

MR. UNPOPULAR
Snappa is not the brainiest Serpent in the Fangpyre tribe, and he is certainly not the most popular. His hot temper and lack of brain power make it hard for the other snakes to like him.

SKALES

HYPNOBRAI GENERAL

THIS COLD AND calculating snake warrior became leader of the Hypnobrai when he beat General Slithraa in a fight. Skales is one of the toughest Serpents and he is skilled in Fang-Kwon-Do, an ancient martial art.

DID YOU KNOW?
There is no love lost between the Serpentine tribes. Yet at one time, the Hypnobrai and Fangpyre tribes were allies, so Skales is very good friends with Fangpyre General Fangtom.

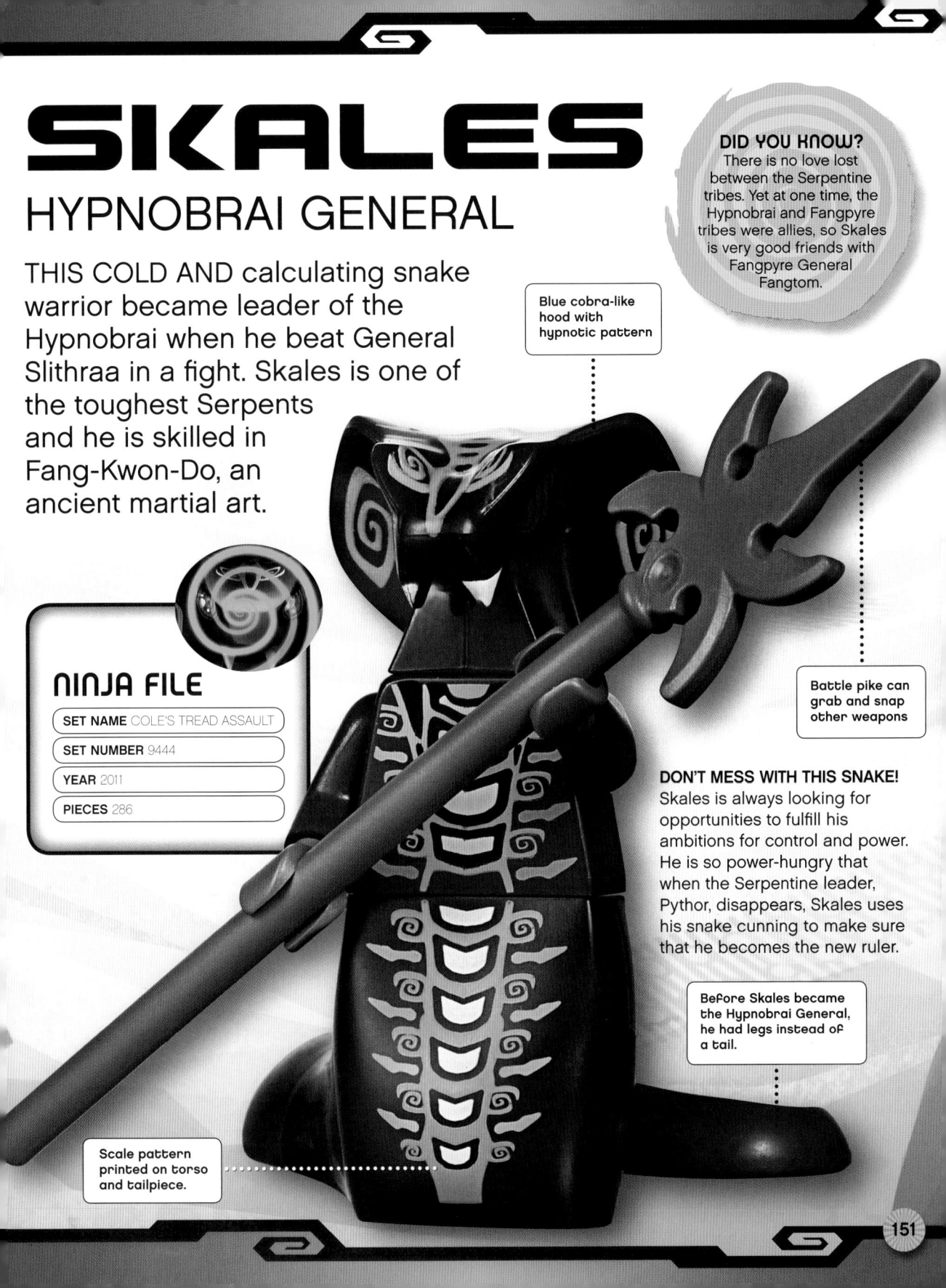

NINJA FILE

SET NAME COLE'S TREAD ASSAULT
SET NUMBER 9444
YEAR 2011
PIECES 286

DON'T MESS WITH THIS SNAKE!
Skales is always looking for opportunities to fulfill his ambitions for control and power. He is so power-hungry that when the Serpentine leader, Pythor, disappears, Skales uses his snake cunning to make sure that he becomes the new ruler.

SLITHRAA

EX HYPNOBRAI GENERAL

SLITHRAA WAS THE head of the Hypnobrai Serpent tribe until he was defeated by his second-in-command, Skales. After this humiliating incident, Slithraa lost his tail and grew legs again.

Unusual bright yellow markings on head

Cobra hood unique to the leaders of each Serpent tribe

Lethal snake fangs

Unique swirling snakeskin patterns on body

NINJA FILE

SET NAME SLITHRAA

SET NUMBER 9573

YEAR 2012

PIECES 20

WEAPONS

HYPNOBRAI STAFF
Owned by the General, this powerful Staff contains the anti-venom to reverse a hypnotic trance.

CHAIN SAI
Swung from a chain, this three-pronged dagger is lethal.

BLUE VIPER
A Hypnobrai minion snake uses mind control to confuse the enemy.

ICY SERPENTS
The Hypnobrai are cobra-like snakes. The tribe was sealed away in the snowy mountains before Lloyd Garmadon accidentally released them. They use hypnosis to control their enemies.

RATTLA

HYPNOBRAI SCOUT

RATTLA IS THE scout for the Hypnobrai Army. He is not known for his brains, but he is loyal and follows orders. He has limited hypnotic powers, but his staff of control makes him very powerful in a fight.

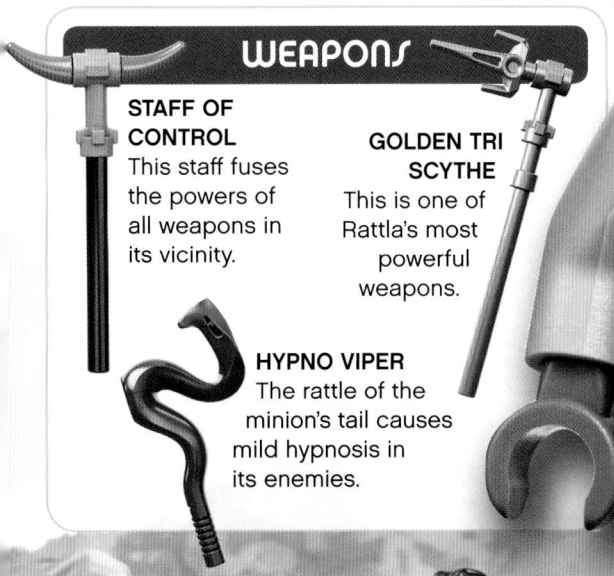

Unique snakeskin pattern begins on top of head

Powerful red-eyed hypnotic stare

Swirling patterns are distinctive of the Hypnobrai tribe.

SINGING SERPENT
Rattla likes to experiment with different ways of confusing his enemies—such as terrible singing or talking them to sleep with boring stories!

NINJA FILE

SET NAME STARTER SET

SET NUMBER 9579

YEAR 2012

PIECES 62

MEZMO

HYPNOBRAI SOLDIER

MEZMO IS A soldier in the Hypnobrai tribe. He is smart and confident—if he doesn't agree with orders, he won't follow them. Mezmo feels he deserves more power in his tribe and should be promoted to a higher rank.

Cobra-shaped head with Hypnobrai markings

Hypnotic eyes

Two large fangs

Blue, yellow, and gray coloring matches other members of the tribe

NINJA FILE

SET NAME MEZMO

SET NUMBER 9555

YEAR 2012

PIECES 31

WEAPONS

GOLDEN DOUBLE AX
This ultimate cutting weapon is made of solid gold!

Golden ax blade

CHAINED FANG
Swing, strike, slice, and smash with this weapon!

PICKAX
This is a handy tool and a lethal weapon.

MESMERIZING!
Mezmo by name, mesmerizing by nature—just don't look into this snake's swirly red eyes. Like all Hypnobrai, he can hypnotize his enemies into doing whatever he wants.

SKALIDOR

CONSTRICTAI GENERAL

NINJA FILE

SET NAME EPIC DRAGON BATTLE

SET NUMBER 9450

YEAR 2012

PIECES 915

SKALIDOR IS the General of the Constrictai tribe. He is plump but powerful, and can crush his enemy with a single blow, or even with the weight of his own body! Ninja—don't be fooled by his size, Skalidor's reflexes are fast!

UNDERGROUND FOE
The Constrictai Serpents live underground in caves and tunnels. When they move above ground the snakes are so heavy they make cracks in the earth—General Skalidor in particular!

BYTAR

CONSTRICTAI WARRIOR

THIS MUSCLE-BOUND warrior is second-in-command in the Constrictai tribe. Bytar is a bully who likes to work out when he isn't fighting. Unfortunately, he doesn't like to wash, so he smells B-A-D! Watch out Ninja, brutish Bytar eats and beats anything!

NINJA FILE

SET NAME BYTAR

SET NUMBER 9556

YEAR 2012

PIECES 25

Distinctive orange spikes on head

Large head with fangs

Vibrant snake scale pattern on torso

Large, muscular arms

WEAPONS

DOUBLE-BLADED SWORD
With this weapon, snakes can achieve twice as much cutting action!

SCYTHE BLADE
This is a lethal heavy metal weapon.

Sharp, curved silver blade

GOLDEN VIPER
Small, but with a mean grip, this viper minion works for the Constrictai.

VICE-LIKE GRIP
The Constrictai are boa constrictor snakes who attack their enemies from underground hideouts and crush them with their vice-like grips.

CHOKUN

CONSTRICTAI SOLDIER

CHOKUN IS A soldier and the protector of the Constrictai tribe. Don't be fooled by his small head, he has huge, sharp fangs. This snake has a killer bite!

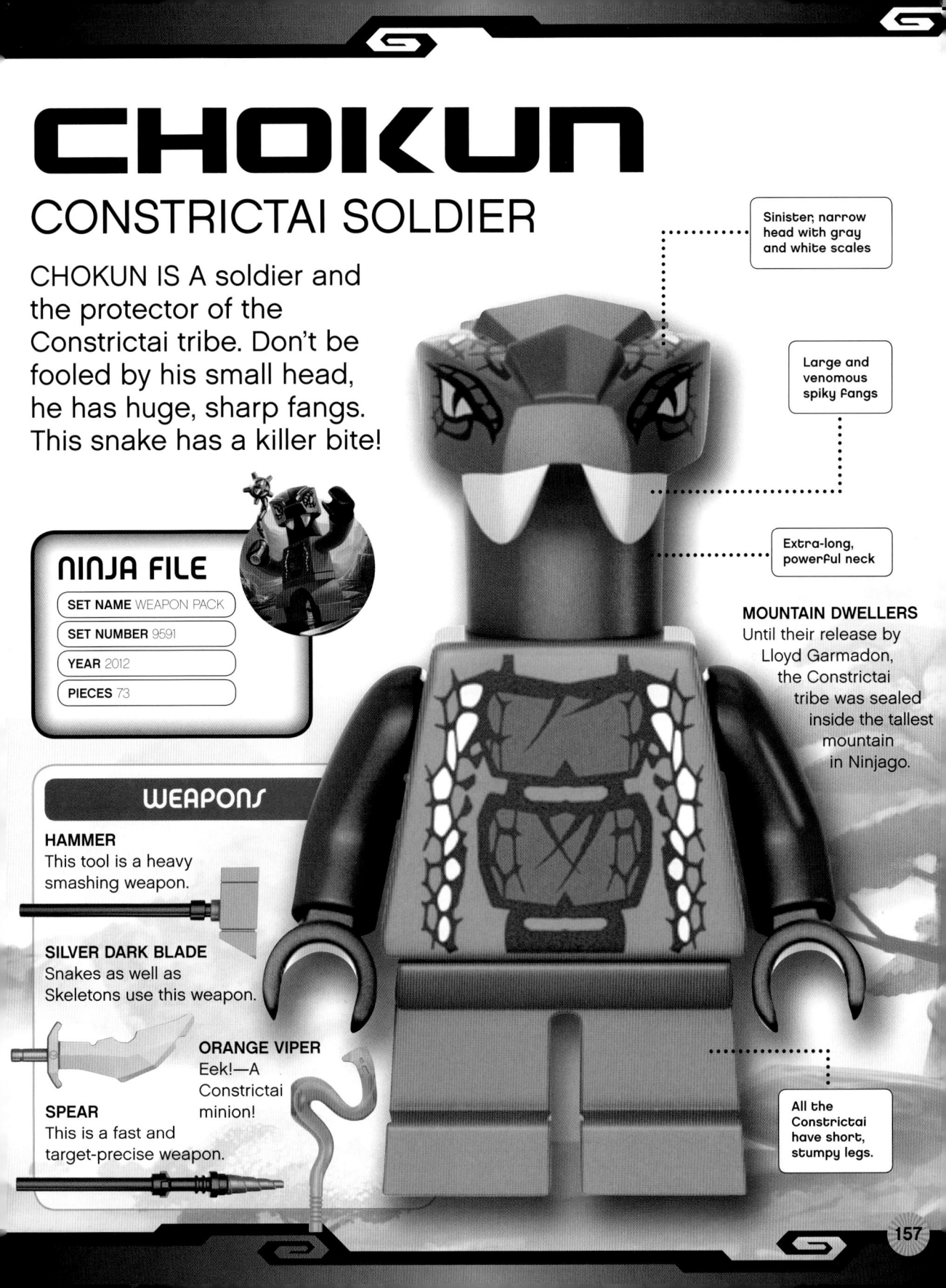

NINJA FILE

SET NAME WEAPON PACK
SET NUMBER 9591
YEAR 2012
PIECES 73

WEAPONS

HAMMER
This tool is a heavy smashing weapon.

SILVER DARK BLADE
Snakes as well as Skeletons use this weapon.

SPEAR
This is a fast and target-precise weapon.

ORANGE VIPER
Eek!—A Constrictai minion!

MOUNTAIN DWELLERS
Until their release by Lloyd Garmadon, the Constrictai tribe was sealed inside the tallest mountain in Ninjago.

SNIKE

CONSTRICTAI SCOUT

SNIKE IS A scout and a sniper in the Constrictai tribe. He is dedicated to his job, but he is slightly cross-eyed and doesn't always hit his targets at the first attempt. Despite this, Snike is confident and thinks he is a skilled sniper.

NINJA FILE

SET NAME SAMURAI MECH

SET NUMBER 9448

YEAR 2012

PIECES 452

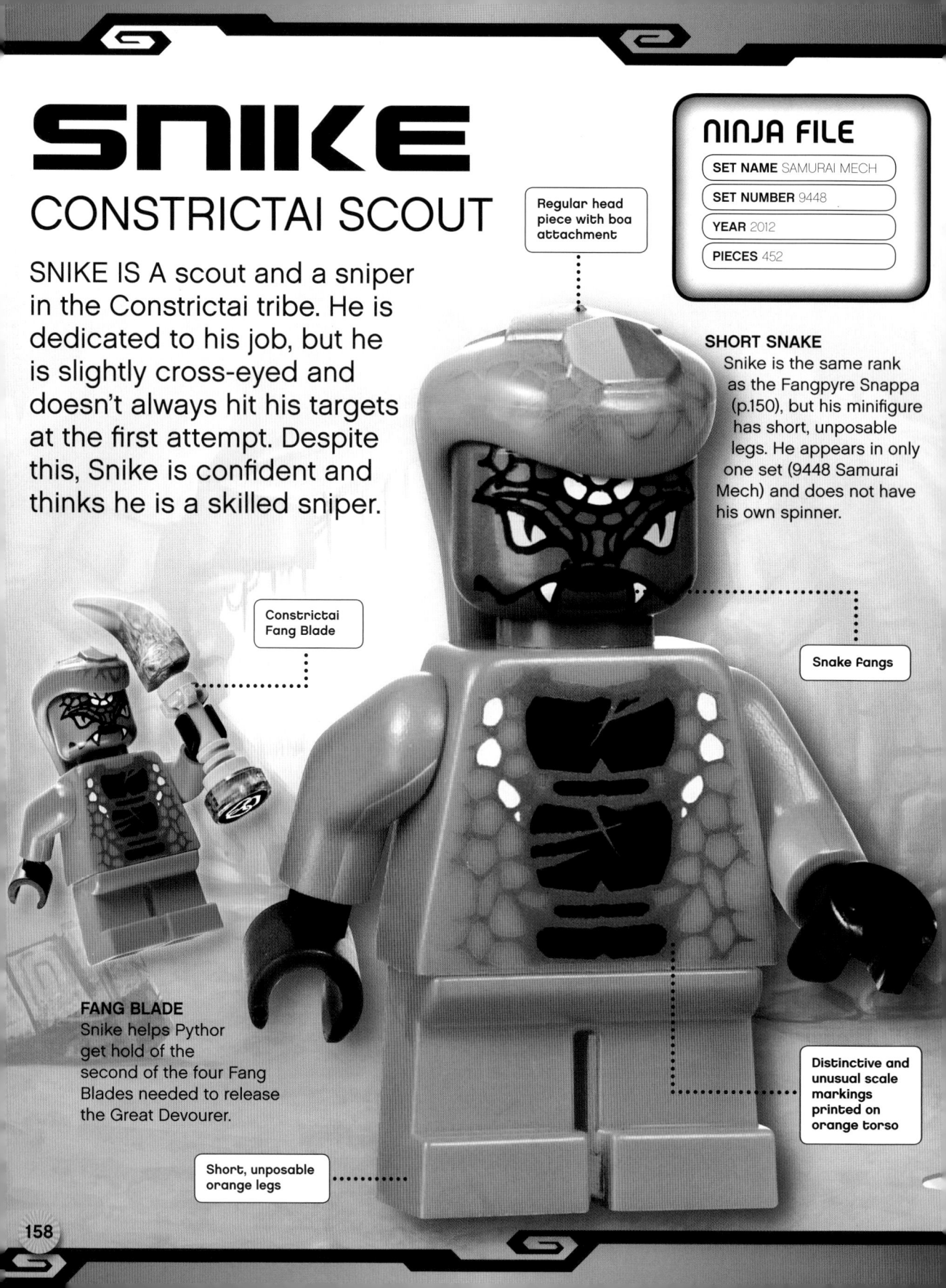

SHORT SNAKE
Snike is the same rank as the Fangpyre Snappa (p.150), but his minifigure has short, unposable legs. He appears in only one set (9448 Samurai Mech) and does not have his own spinner.

FANG BLADE
Snike helps Pythor get hold of the second of the four Fang Blades needed to release the Great Devourer.

PYTHOR

LAST OF THE ANACONDRAI

PYTHOR WAS GENERAL of the villainous Anacondrai, but now he is the tribe's last surviving member. He is the King of the Serpentine. Pythor wants all four Fang Blades so that he can release the Great Devourer and destroy Ninjago.

NINJA FILE

SET NAME ULTRA SONIC RAIDER

SET NUMBER 9449

YEAR 2012

PIECES 622

DID YOU KNOW?
Pythor, also known as Pythor P. Chumsworth, is exclusive to set 9449 (Ultra Sonic Raider). This set also features the ZX versions for the four Ninja and Spitta from the Venomari tribe.

Open-mouthed head with four fangs is unique

Scale pattern printed on uniquely purple torso, neck, and head

Red vial of venom attached to handle of the Fangpyre Fang Blade

Long snake tail typical of all Serpent Generals

PRIDE COMES BEFORE A FALL!
When Pythor finally gets his hands on all four Fang Blades, he places them in the statue of the Great Devourer in order to release him from his tomb under the Lost City of Oroboris. His moment of triumph is short-lived—the first thing the Great Devourer does after his release is devour Pythor!

SNAKE ARENA

KAI VS. RATTLA

COME TO THE Snake Arena for an awesome Spinjitzu battle between Ninja Kai and Serpent Rattla. Kai is dressed in his Kendo outfit and must use his new Kendo skills to defeat the icy Rattla. Kai wields the Fire Dragon Sword, while the evil Serpent is aided by a hypnotic snake head.

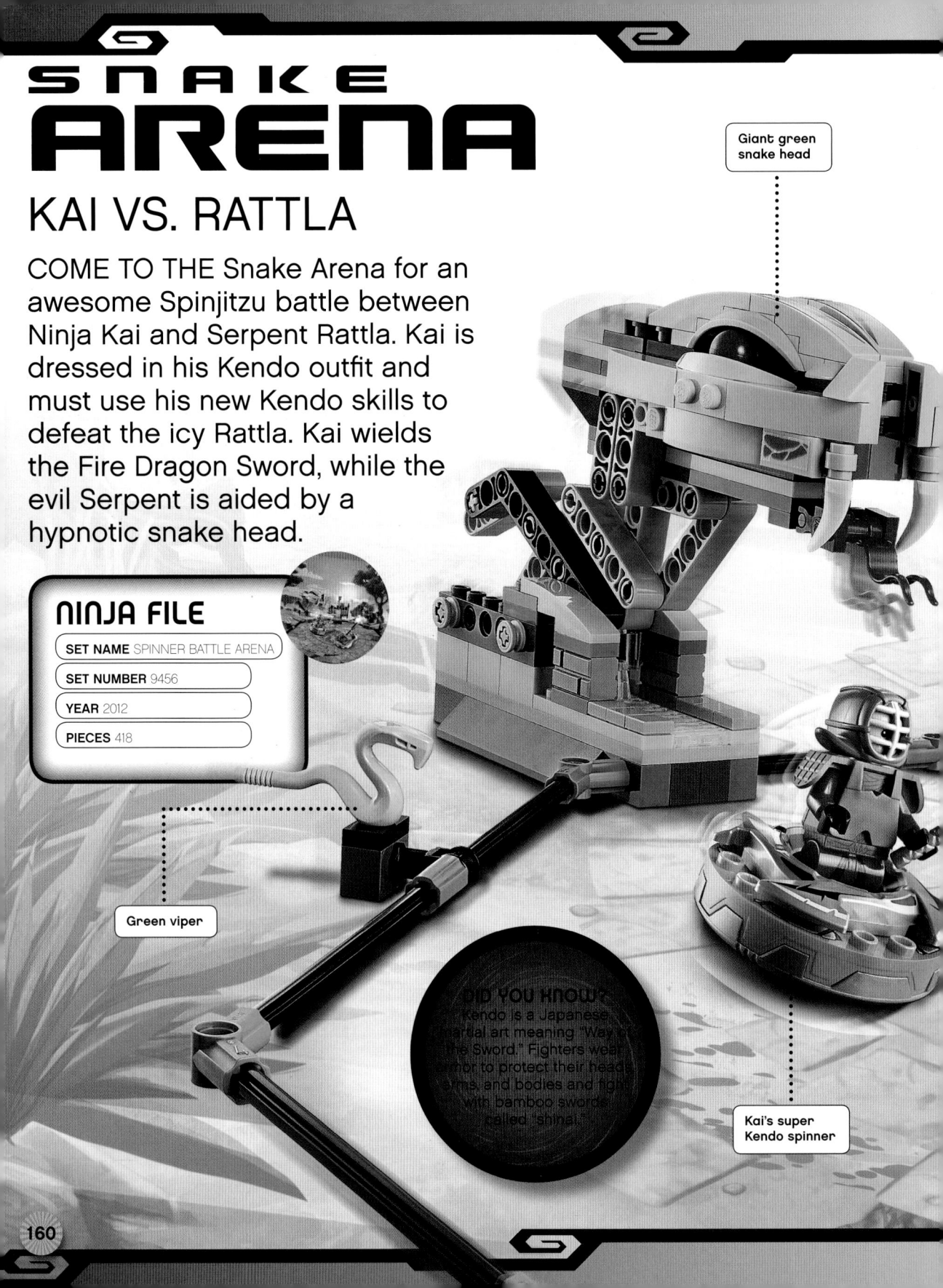

NINJA FILE

SET NAME SPINNER BATTLE ARENA

SET NUMBER 9456

YEAR 2012

PIECES 418

DID YOU KNOW?

Kendo is a Japanese martial art meaning "Way of the Sword." Fighters wear armor to protect their heads, arms, and bodies and fight with bamboo swords called "shinai."

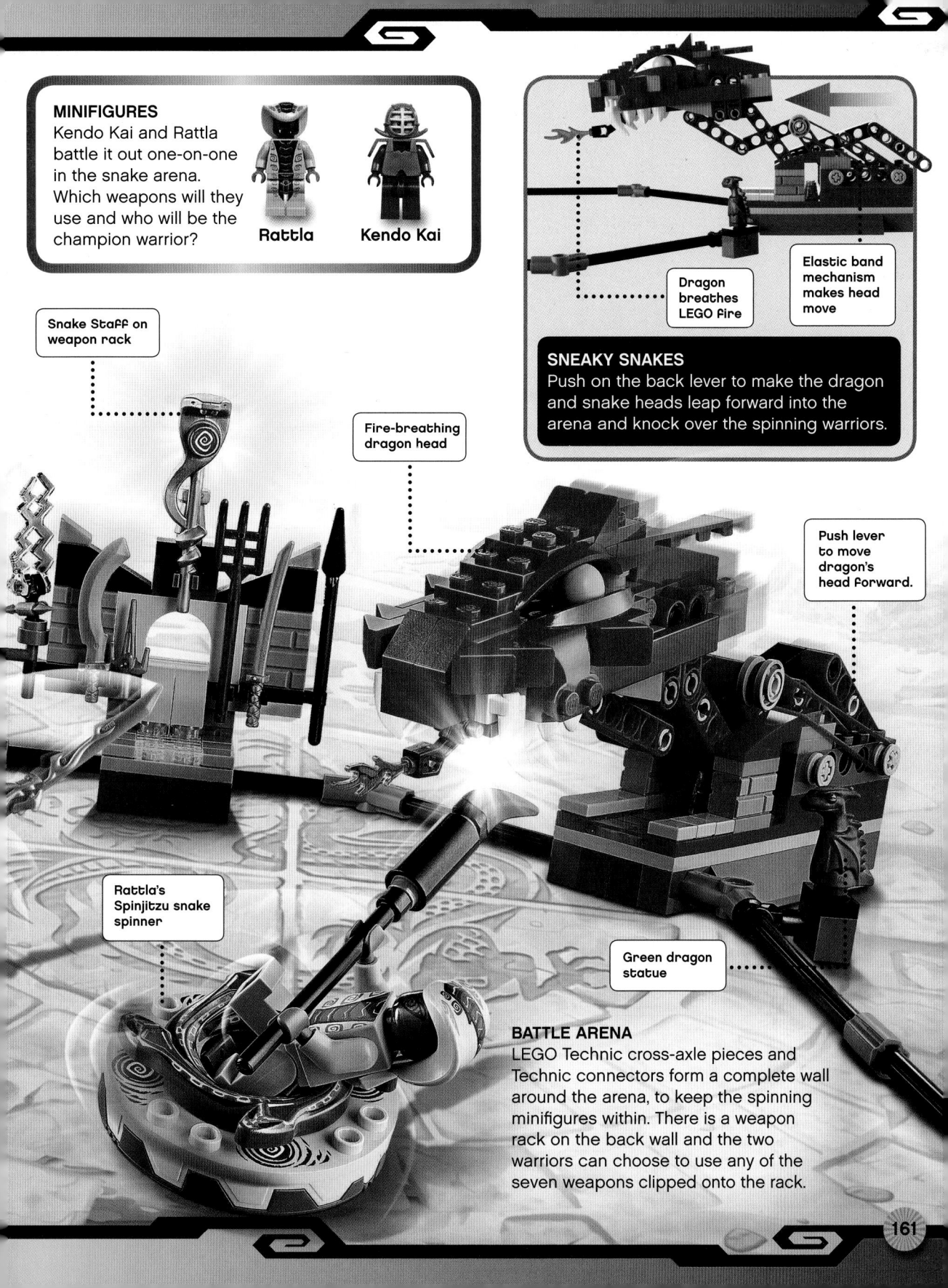

MINIFIGURES
Kendo Kai and Rattla battle it out one-on-one in the snake arena. Which weapons will they use and who will be the champion warrior?

SNEAKY SNAKES
Push on the back lever to make the dragon and snake heads leap forward into the arena and knock over the spinning warriors.

BATTLE ARENA
LEGO Technic cross-axle pieces and Technic connectors form a complete wall around the arena, to keep the spinning minifigures within. There is a weapon rack on the back wall and the two warriors can choose to use any of the seven weapons clipped onto the rack.

EPIC DRAGON BATTLE

GOOD VS. EVIL

SENSEI WU HAS been captured by the Serpentine Army and the Great Devourer is on the loose. The Green Ninja and the Ultra Dragon—the most powerful of all Dragons—must defeat this evil beast, while Jay uses Zen skills to battle the snakes. Even Lord Garmadon is on the Ninja's side. Let battle commence!

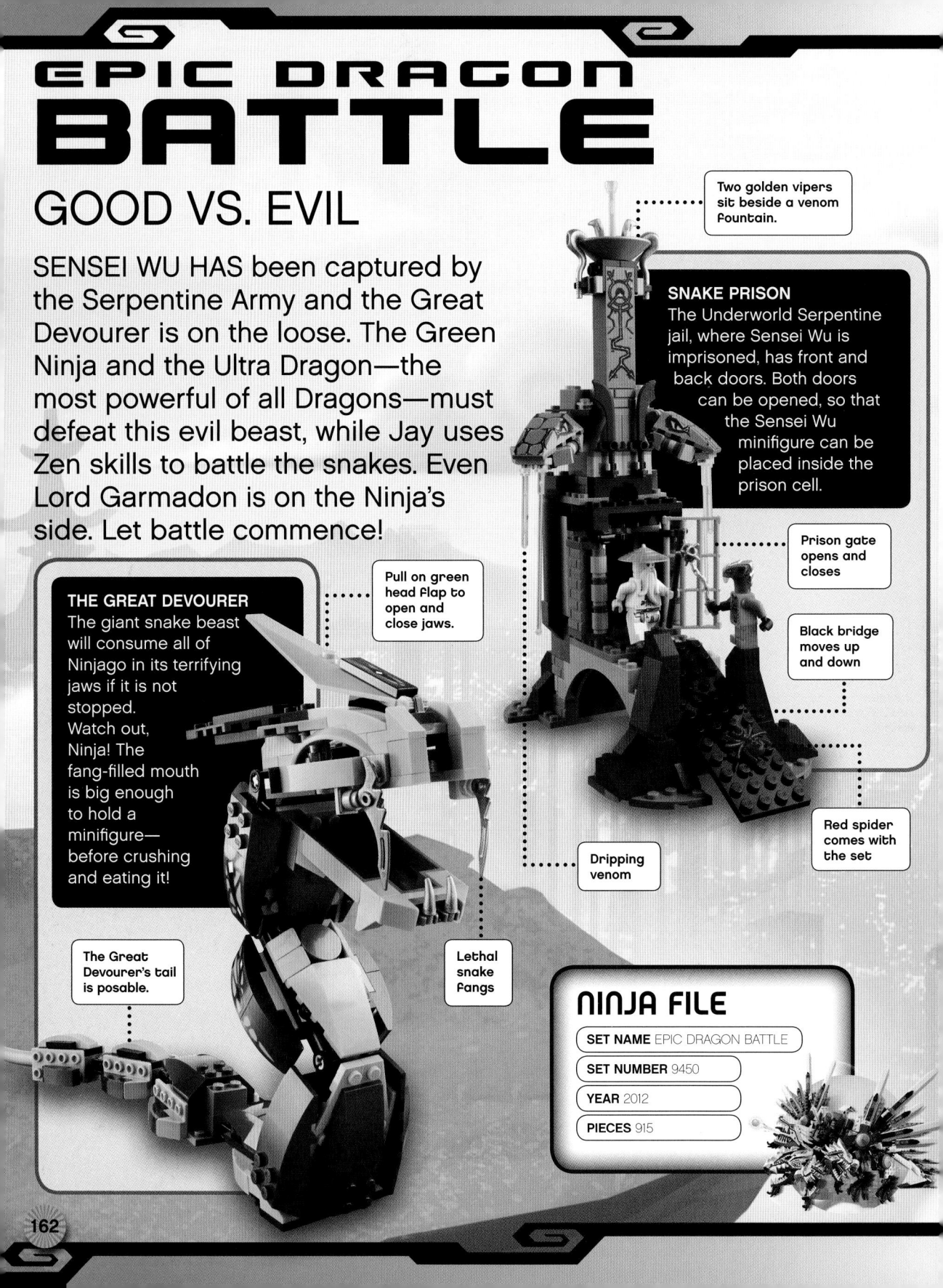

SNAKE PRISON
The Underworld Serpentine jail, where Sensei Wu is imprisoned, has front and back doors. Both doors can be opened, so that the Sensei Wu minifigure can be placed inside the prison cell.

THE GREAT DEVOURER
The giant snake beast will consume all of Ninjago in its terrifying jaws if it is not stopped. Watch out, Ninja! The fang-filled mouth is big enough to hold a minifigure—before crushing and eating it!

NINJA FILE

SET NAME EPIC DRAGON BATTLE
SET NUMBER 9450
YEAR 2012
PIECES 915

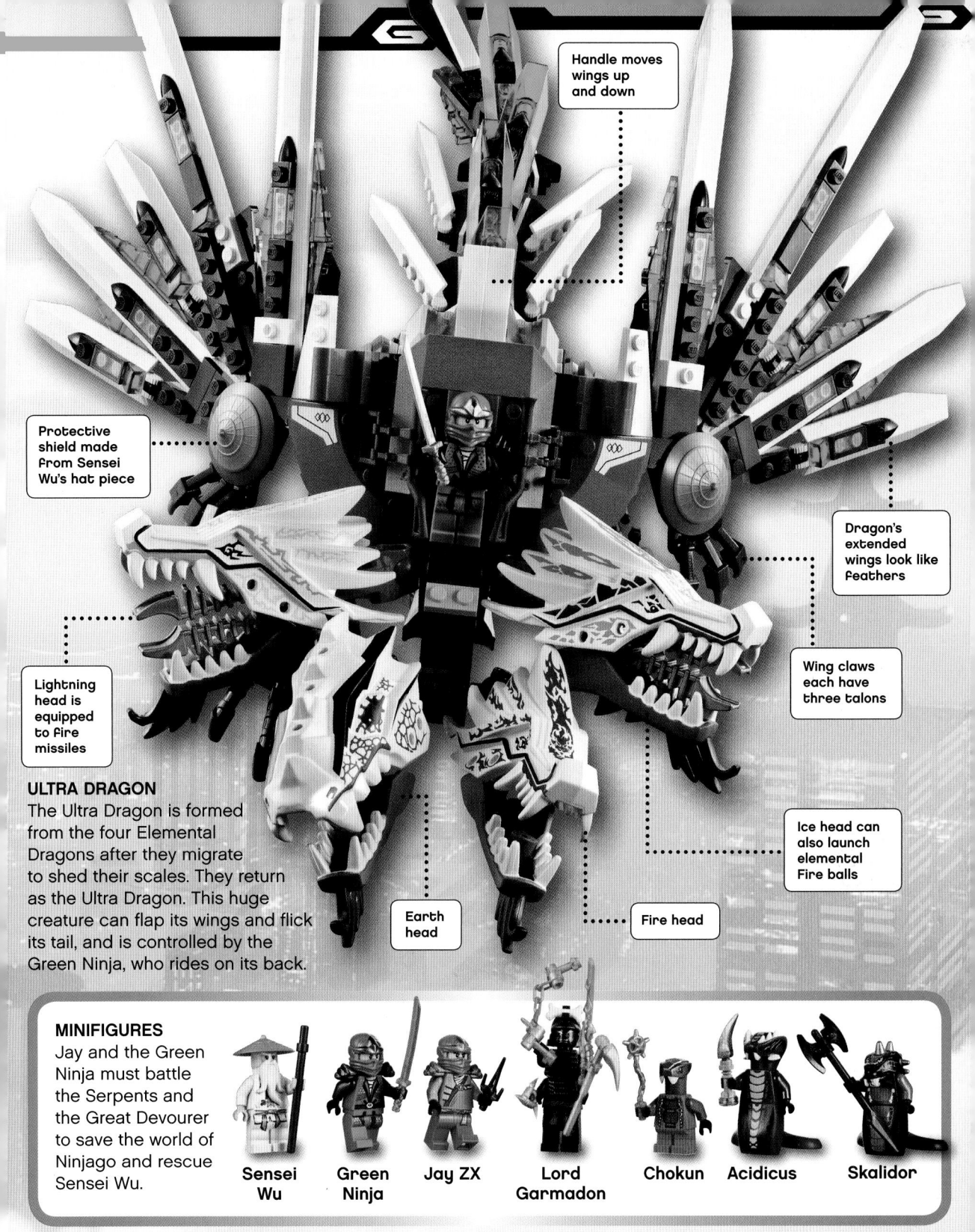

ULTRA DRAGON
The Ultra Dragon is formed from the four Elemental Dragons after they migrate to shed their scales. They return as the Ultra Dragon. This huge creature can flap its wings and flick its tail, and is controlled by the Green Ninja, who rides on its back.

MINIFIGURES
Jay and the Green Ninja must battle the Serpents and the Great Devourer to save the world of Ninjago and rescue Sensei Wu.

WEAPONS

TAKE A LOOK at some fantastic weapons! Both the Ninja and the Serpentine use this amazing arsenal to attack their foes. While the Ninja prefer traditional swords, daggers, and, of course, their Golden Weapons, the Serpentine use a terrifying array of vile, venom-filled weapons.

SWORDS AND KNIVES

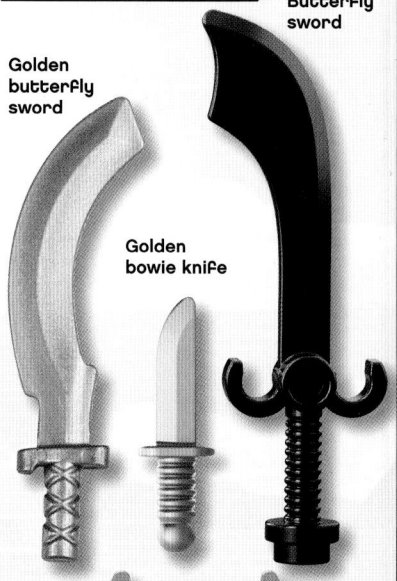

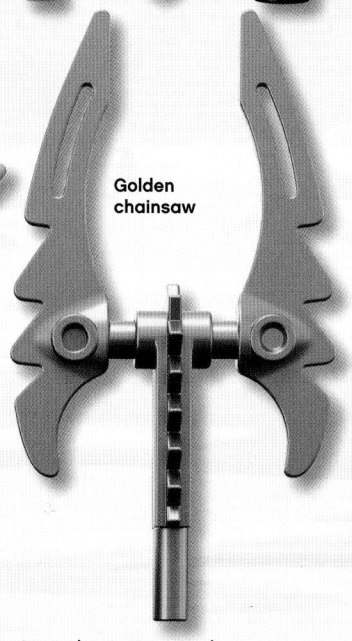

Don't underestimate these ornate blades—they're beautiful but also extremely sharp.

CHAINED WEAPONS

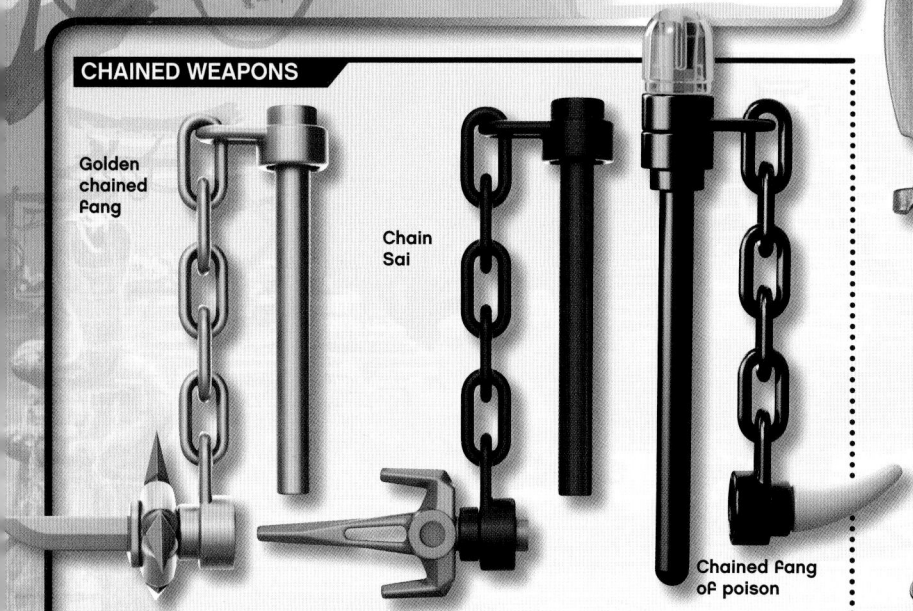

Watch out for these swinging spikes. Some are venomous, and some have more than one blade, but all of them are dangerous!

HAMMERS

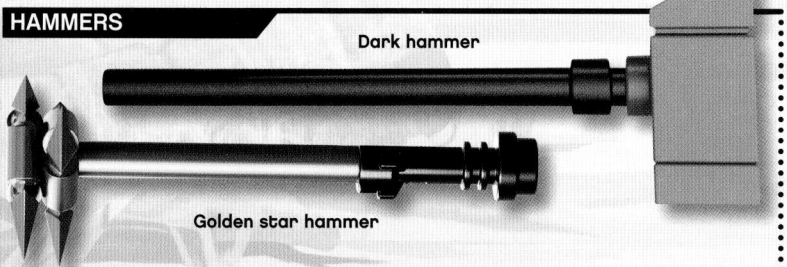

Only the strongest minifigure can lift these heavy weapons, let alone do battle with them.

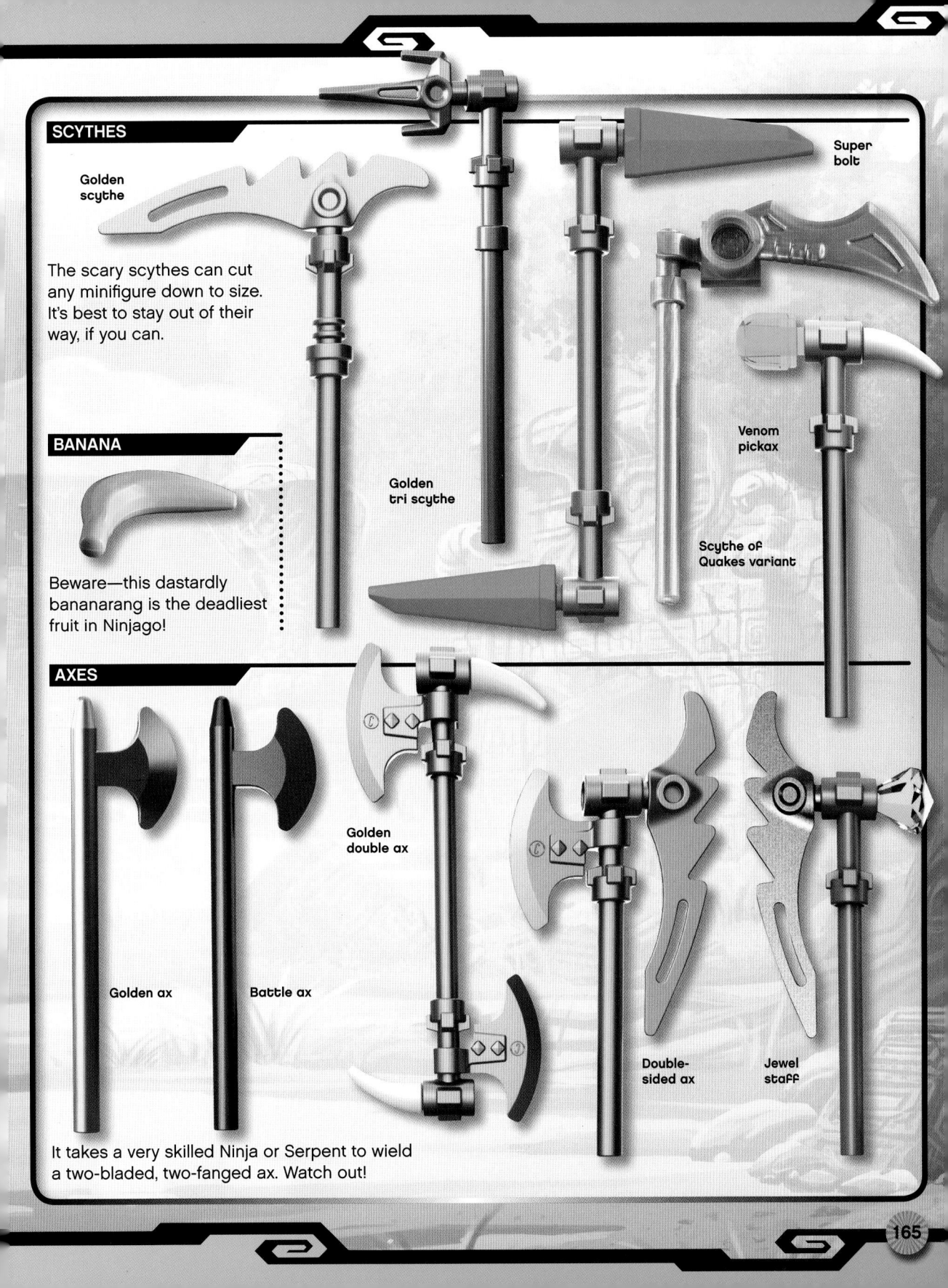
SCYTHES
Golden scythe
Super bolt
The scary scythes can cut any minifigure down to size. It's best to stay out of their way, if you can.
Venom pickax
Golden tri scythe
Scythe of Quakes variant
BANANA
Beware—this dastardly bananarang is the deadliest fruit in Ninjago!
AXES
Golden double ax
Golden ax
Battle ax
Double-sided ax
Jewel staff
It takes a very skilled Ninja or Serpent to wield a two-bladed, two-fanged ax. Watch out!

STAFFS

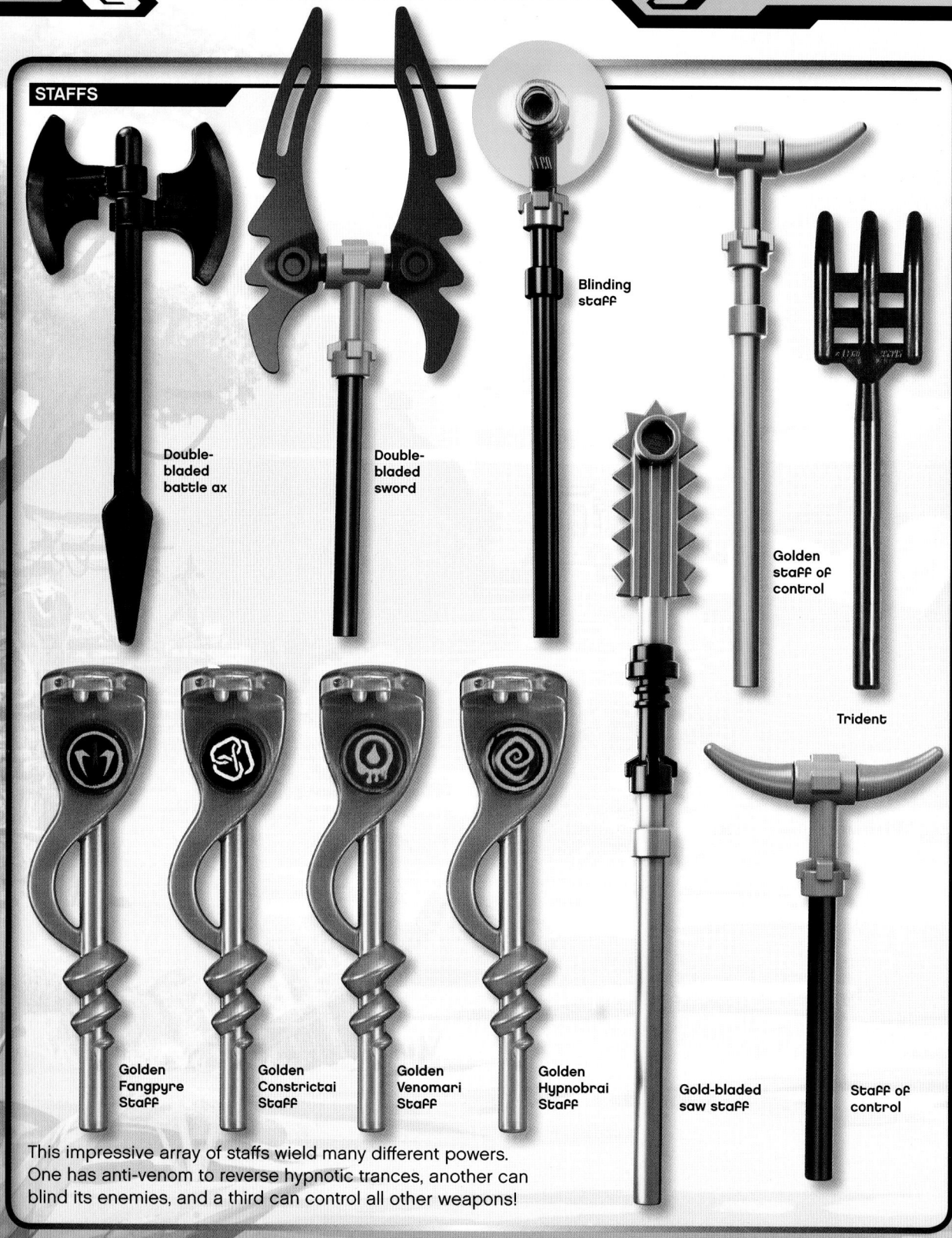

This impressive array of staffs wield many different powers. One has anti-venom to reverse hypnotic trances, another can blind its enemies, and a third can control all other weapons!

FANG BLADES

Made from pure silver and vials of anti-venom, these weapons are extremely powerful.

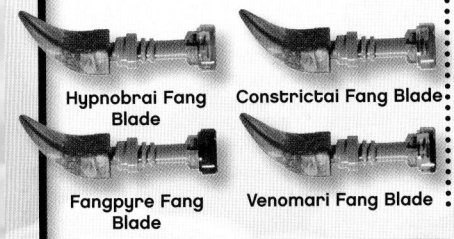

STRIKERS

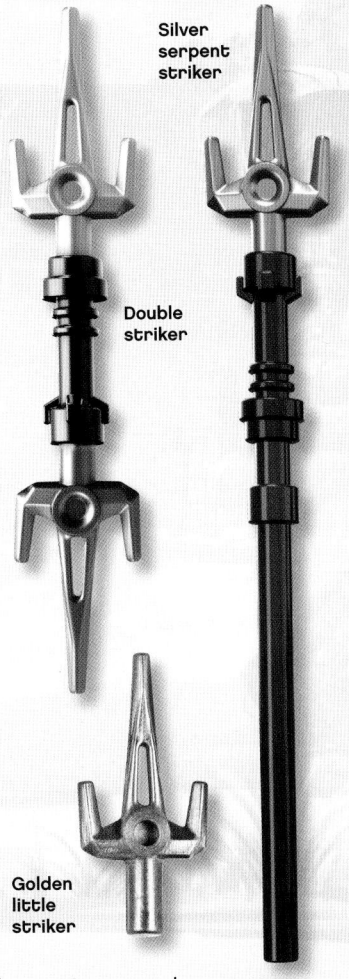

These tri-pronged weapons can be used in close combat or thrown from a distance.

SPEARS

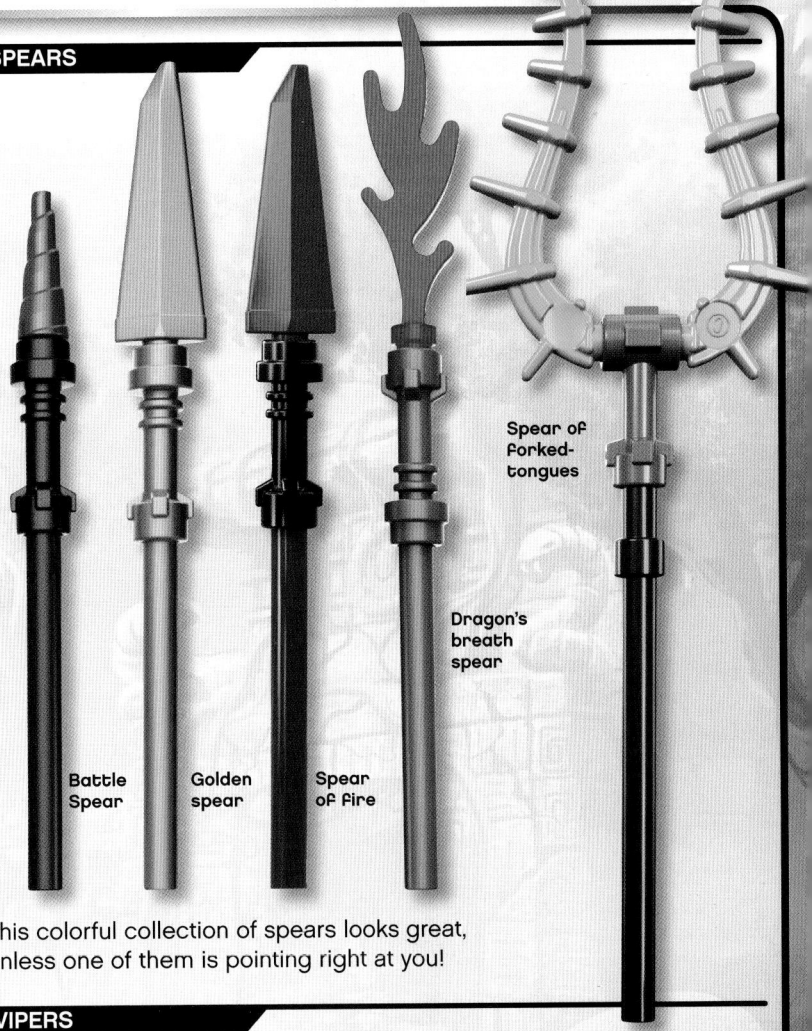

This colorful collection of spears looks great, unless one of them is pointing right at you!

VIPERS

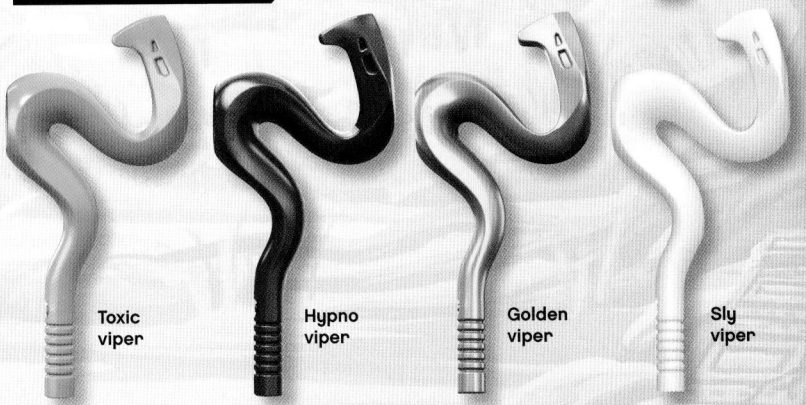

Whether they are shaking their noisy rattles, oozing with poison, or letting off smelly stink bombs, these slithery snake weapons are all ssscary!

ULTRA DRAGON VS. THE GREAT DEVOURER

AN EPIC BATTLE between good and evil is about to take place. The Serpents capture Sensei Wu, and finally unleash the Great Devourer. The Ninja call on the Green Ninja, the Ultra Dragon, and their enemy, Lord Garmadon, to help...

RESCUE! The Ninja find Sensei Wu. He tells them that Lloyd is the Green Ninja, and that Lloyd and Lord Garmadon are the only ones who can destroy the Great Devourer. Can either of them be trusted?

Lord Garmadon wields the Four Golden Weapons.

Serpentine prison cell

HERO! The Green Ninja arrives with the Ultra Dragon to join the battle. The Ninja combine their elemental powers to control the Great Devourer just long enough for Garmadon to deliver the fatal blow with the four Golden Weapons. So long, snake!
Only the Green Ninja can control the Ultra Dragon.
DONE! The Great Devourer is destroyed and Ninjago is saved! But Garmadon has disappeared with the Golden Weapons. Has he gone back over to the Underworld? Only time will tell...

AND BEYOND...

HAVING DEFEATED THE Skeleton Army and the Serpentine, the Ninja will soon be ready to face a new challenge. In the meantime, turn the page to discover all the information you could ever need about all the LEGO® Ninjago sets and minifigures. Go in peace Ninja warrior!

MINIFIGURE GALLERY

WHO IS YOUR favorite LEGO Ninjago minifigure? Is it Nya with her double-sided face, the two-headed Fangtom and Fangdam, or the super-short Lloyd Garmadon? Check out this line-up of all the amazing minifigures and make your choice!

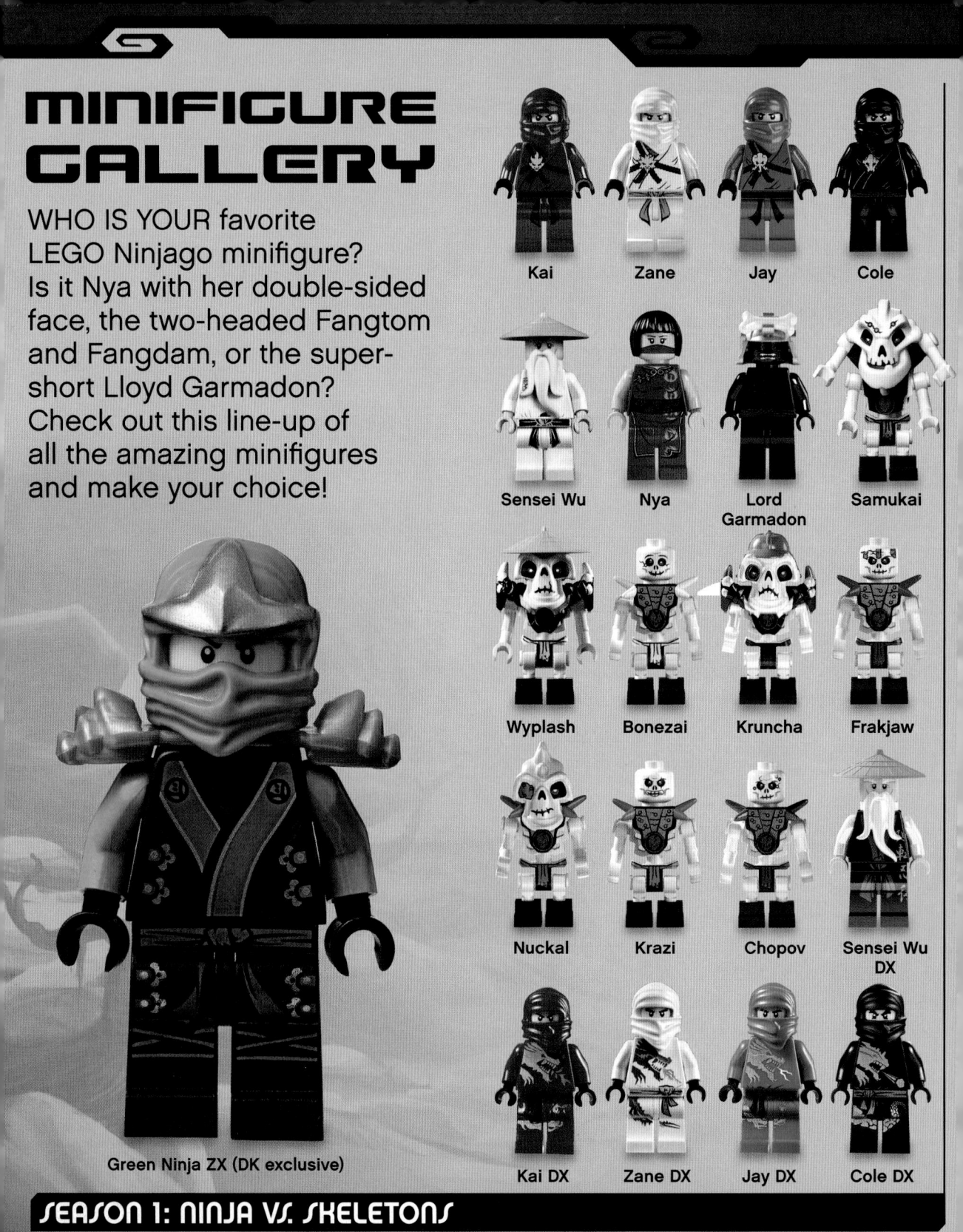

Green Ninja ZX (DK exclusive)

SEASON 2: NINJA VS. SERPENTINES

SET GALLERY

HERE ARE ALL the LEGO® Ninjago sets produced so far in each series. How many sets have you collected? Which one is your favorite? Look out for even more sets coming in 2013!

2516 Ninja Training Outpost

2507 Fire Temple

2519 Skeleton Bowling

2509 Earth Dragon Defence

2263 Turbo Shredder

2518 Nuckal's ATV

2505 Garmadon's Dark Fortress

2521 Lightning Dragon Battle

2260 Ice Dragon Attack

2504 Spinjitzu Dojo

2506 Skull Truck

2254 Mountain Shrine

2259 Skull Motorbike

2258 Ninja Ambush

2520 Ninjago Battle Arena

2508 Blacksmith Shop

SEASON 1: NINJA VS. SKELETONS